The Most Offensive Book Ever Written

The Most Offensive Book Ever Written

TIM DUSTIN

RESOURCE *Publications* • Eugene, Oregon

THE MOST OFFENSIVE BOOK EVER WRITTEN

Copyright © 2022 Tim Dustin. All rights reserved. Except for brief quotations in critical publications or reviews, no part of this book may be reproduced in any manner without prior written permission from the publisher. Write: Permissions, Wipf and Stock Publishers, 199 W. 8th Ave., Suite 3, Eugene, OR 97401.

Resource Publications
An Imprint of Wipf and Stock Publishers
199 W. 8th Ave., Suite 3
Eugene, OR 97401

www.wipfandstock.com

PAPERBACK ISBN: 978-1-6667-4742-3
HARDCOVER ISBN: 978-1-6667-4743-0
EBOOK ISBN: 978-1-6667-4744-7

VERSION NUMBER 072222

For You, God.
May Your truth be revealed in this work, and not mine.

Contents

Note | ix

Welcome to the Arena | 1

Homosexuality | 5

Gay Marriage | 11

Abortion | 16

Drinking | 21

Divorce | 25

The Death Penalty | 31

Heterosexual Marriage | 36

Pornography | 41

Intermission | 46

Politics | 49

Forgiveness | 56

Pre-Marital Sex | 61

Human Idols | 66

Other Religions | 71

Heaven | 77

Hell | 83

Jesus | 89

In Closing | 99

Acknowledgements | 107

Note

Some capitalization and italicizing has been added to certain verses for emphasis by discretion of the author. All verses are from the New International Version (NIV) Bible translation.

- Matthew 28:19–20a: "Therefore go and make disciples of all nations, baptizing them in the name of the Father and of the Son and of the Holy Spirit, and teaching them to obey *everything* I have commanded you."

- Romans 1:16a: "I am not ashamed of the gospel, because it is the power of God for the salvation of everyone who believes."

- Hebrews 6:19a: "We have this hope as an anchor for the soul, firm and secure."

- 1 John 2:15: "Do not love the world or anything in the world. If anyone loves the world, the love of the Father is not in him."

Welcome to the Arena

In the early 1900s, miners started taking cages of canaries into the coal mines with them. Canaries are more sensitive to certain poisonous gasses than people are, so when a canary would die down in the mines, it'd be a warning to the miners to evacuate; it could mean their lives were in danger. The canaries acted as an upcoming poster for devastation ahead.

Let this book be a canary in the coal mine.

The Catcher in the Rye, Animal Farm, Lolita, The Grapes of Wrath, and *Ulysses* are just a few titles among the countless number of books that have been banned over the years. They were banned for profanity, graphic content, language, and political leanings, but have since seen the light of day and become classics in their own right.

In today's culture, there are still many Hell-bent on canceling any works they see as "offensive." Certain sects of society are pushing to a place where anything offensive (in their eyes) is banned, canceled, and off-limits. I'm here to say it's only a matter of time before cancel culture comes after the most offensive book ever written: the Bible.

We're living in the time of mega churches and mega pastors. Many people don't own physical Bibles (or open them), let alone encounter scripture or verses outside of twenty minute McSermons used to encourage, inspire, and keep you coming back week after week. Churches are becoming less about scripture and truth and more about pleasing the masses. Now, don't get me wrong, there are many churches that preach Bible-based teachings, but it's often to congregations small enough to meet in basements, not stadiums.

Many who identify as Christians now-a-days say they believe in Jesus, but don't know what that *actually* means; they say they believe in the Bible, but they don't know what's in it. Ask them, "What does the Bible say about abortion? Pre-marital sex? Gay marriage?" Many churches are coming up short when it comes down to teaching the gritty truths of the Bible. Too many congregations have a sole purpose of "feeling good;" they don't want to look at the sins they're leading in their own lives.

Second Timothy 3:16 says, "All scripture is God-breathed and is useful for teaching, rebuking, correcting, and training in righteousness." It doesn't say "some scripture;" it says "*all.*" We're going to get into some deep waters, and that can be uncomfortable, but discomfort can be good in pushing us to something greater. Like working out, you get stronger when you gradually push yourself harder. And that's what we're going to do together. We're going to get our hands dirty and read what the Bible says and study its truths together.

But before we go any further, let me be perfectly clear: I'm not here to wag my finger at anybody. I, too, am a sinner saved by grace. In 1 Timothy 1:15, Paul writes, "Here is a trustworthy saying that deserves full acceptance: Christ Jesus came into the world to save sinners—of whom I am the worst." And that's me. I've committed millions of sins in my lifetime. I'm no better than *anyone*. I write the following pages with a heart of extreme grace and honest truth.

I'm not writing to purposefully lunge at anyone's throat; we're all imperfect people living in this imperfect world. I want to take what the Bible says and teach it so we can apply it in our lives as it should be applied, and not ignored. Many churches are not doing their jobs. They are not preaching *all* scripture. Their preaching may be implied, milky, or absent all-together. So, what we're going to do, we're going to read scripture word-for-word and see what it has to say, first in the Old Testament and then the New Testament.

Welcome to the Arena

Note I'm not an ordained pastor, preacher, or counselor. I'm someone who loves God, Jesus, and the Bible. I'm also someone who has worked in the church world and has heard what sermons are being taught. If church leaders aren't going to say it, then the responsibility falls on us—the Christian Body—to spread the truth found between the Bible's covers.

Let's dive into the Bible, maybe some of you for the very first time, and see what it actually says; we hear podcasts, scroll through social media, and listen to summaries, but let's go to the source of sources and read its words; let's find the truth in the Bible, which today's society might find incredibly offensive due to its conservative, moral, and "alienating" nature.

My hope is when you're finished reading this work of mine, you'll feel enlightened and stronger in your faith. Some of these chapters might be brutal and challenging, but if following Christ was easy, He never would have told us to take up our crosses (Matthew 16:24). Let's test the depths of our faith because it's eternally important. Let's be the kind of Christians that don't shy away, but go head-first into the fray. Let's teach ourselves, learn, and apply through abundant mercy and God-given wisdom, because being a Believer of Jesus is not simple work.

And, before we get started, whoever you are and wherever you're at, know Jesus loves you. It doesn't matter who you are, what you've done, what your life is like, or what kind of mess you're living—Jesus loves you right where you're at. And that's why you can face these upcoming chapters, because you're loved no matter what. If you identify with a topic and start to feel some conviction, *that's okay*. Welcome to the club! Jesus doesn't love you any less. It's because of His love we're able to open the pages of His Word and humbly learn where we can grow.

> This is love: not that we loved God, but that He loved us and sent His Son as an atoning sacrifice for our sins. (1 John 4:10)

Let's pray:

Father God, I'm so thankful I know You. I'm so thankful for Your unending mercy and grace, a mercy and grace I need every day for my impatience, lust, critical tongue, and anger. Thank You for Your undeserved love.

I want to pray for my friends reading this—whoever they are and wherever they're at. I ask You show them who You are during this time together, that You're a God of justice and righteousness, but also a God of peace, joy, and amazing, amazing love.

I ask Your words be spoken—not mine. I ask for the ability to balance hard topics with truth and gentleness.

Help us not to judge, but to welcome. Help us not to shut down, but be open to what Your Word says about who You are and what You ask of us. Help us see You not as a shaking fist, but as Your open arms on the cross.

You are God and You are eternally good. May Your will be done—here—in this place, right now.

Amen.

All right, y'all, let's get into it . . .

Homosexuality

The Old Testament

- Genesis 19:4–7: "Before they had gone to bed, all the men from every part of the city of Sodom—both young and old—surrounded the house. They called to Lot, 'Where are the men who came to you tonight? Bring them out to us so that we can have sex with them.' Lot went outside to meet them and said, 'No, my friends. Don't do this wicked thing.'"
- Leviticus 18:22: "Do not lie with a man as one lies with a woman; that is detestable."
- Leviticus 20:13: "If a man lies with a man as one lies with a woman, both of them have done what is detestable."

See also Genesis 19:1–29 for complete context on the story of Sodom and Gomorrah.

The New Testament

- Romans 1:27: "In the same way the men also abandoned natural relations with women and were inflamed with lust for one another. Men committed indecent acts with other men, and received in themselves the due penalty for their perversion."
- 1 Corinthians 6:9: "Do you not know that the wicked will not inherit the kingdom of God? Do not be deceived: Neither

the sexually immoral nor idolaters nor adulterers nor male prostitutes nor homosexual offenders."

- Ephesians 5:3: "But among you there must not be even a hint of sexual immorality, or any kind of impurity, or greed, because these are improper for the Lord's people."
- 1 Timothy 1:8–11: "We know that the law is good if one uses it properly. We also know that the law is made not for the righteous but for lawbreakers and rebels, the ungodly and sinful, the unholy and irreligious, for those who kill their fathers or mothers, for murderers, for the sexually immoral, for those practicing homosexuality, for slave traders and liars and perjurers. And it is for whatever else is contrary to the sound doctrine that conforms to the gospel concerning the glory of the blessed God, which He entrusted me."

See also 1 Timothy 1:3–7 for complete context of the previous passage; extremely applicable today.

We're going to hit the ground running.

There is not one instance *in all of scripture* where a same-sex relationship is looked on in a positive light.

I'm sure for some of you, reading the verses at the beginning of this section might have been a little rattling. Maybe you've been told one thing and shown another. That's okay! I'm glad you're reading. We're going to talk through the tough topics and break them down. Hang with me.

And if you're part of the LGBTQ community, I don't want you to have read the previous verses and think, "God hates gays, so He hates me." No. God loves you so much He sent His Son to die on the cross for you (Luke 5:31–32). You are loved more than you know. Please know that as we continue on.

For many, this is often where the conversation stops, right? "Okay, I see the verses. God hates gays. I'm going to move on and forget God because He represents oppression and punishment." But a critical question often overlooked here is this: *why?* Why doesn't God approve of homosexuality? The "why" is what's so important in *all* of these topics.

So, why isn't homosexuality acceptable to God? Let's look at the beginning:

> So the man gave names to all the livestock, the birds of the air and all the beasts of the field. But for Adam no suitable helper was found. So the Lord God caused the man to fall into a deep sleep; and while he was sleeping, He took one of man's ribs and closed up the place with flesh. Then the Lord God made a woman from the rib He had taken out of the man, and He brought her to the man.
>
> The man said, "This is now bone of my bones and flesh of my flesh; she shall be called 'woman,' for she was taken out of man."
>
> For this reason a man will leave his father and mother and be united with his wife, and they will become one flesh. (Genesis 2:20–24)

I know society and the world are saying a lot right now about gender roles and men and women, that they're the same, can do the same things, and that they're basically interchangeable. God's reality is not ours, though: He created man and woman to be different.

Looking at those verses in Genesis 2, we see man—alone. God placed man in the Garden of Eden to work and take care of it (Genesis 2:15). But man was alone and there was no partner for him. Seeing man alone, with no suitable partner, God created woman.

God created woman to be the *perfect* partner for man. They balance each other out. One excels here, the other there. They were created to be a team that could multiply and flourish (Genesis 1:28).

In the beginning, God could have created another man and had a singular sex, but He didn't. He created a partner for Adam who was completely different from him: Eve.

In addition, in those verses, we see a marriage—a man leaving his parents to be united with his wife. We'll talk more about marriage in following sections, but in the second chapter of the Bible we see a singular man and a singular woman, both created with the other in mind, to work together and partner as a team. We don't see two men or two women. We see God's perfect plan and design: heterosexual marriage.

Being a born-again Christian, the Bible is my rock. I've had to make some difficult decisions in my life based on what the Bible says. The Bible is never-changing. It's God's Word and I completely believe that. Because of what it says, I didn't have sex before marriage (almost impossible in today's society), I'm pro-life even when it comes to the death penalty (even though in my heart I want punishment and justice), and I have a firm belief that Hell is real (but I want everyone to see Heaven). As a human, made of flesh, my worldly side doesn't always want to agree with what the Bible says, but I believe what the Bible says. The world's beliefs change—*literally*—every day. Politics and convenience drive decisions. The Bible, however, in one form or another, has been rock solid for thousands of years, and that's where my beliefs come from. If the Bible says something, then yeah, I believe it, no matter what the world affirms.

I believe homosexuality is a sin based on what the Bible says (see previously referenced verses 1 Corinthians 6:9, Ephesians 5:3, and 1 Timothy 1:8–11). Again, homosexuality is never—not once—described in the Bible in an acceptable, positive light.

Now, here comes a hard question for many: then why did God make me this way? *Why* did God make me LGBTQ?

Stay with me: I don't believe He did. I don't see scientific research that supports humans being born LGBTQ. Instead, I see homosexuality stemming from exterior sources, not interior ones—a learned behavior.

For example: I grew up in a dysfunctional home. Because of the dysfunction I was surrounded with, I learned certain behaviors to cope and survive—manipulation, passive aggressiveness, codependency, and people-pleasing. I don't believe anyone is necessarily born with those traits, but they're learned through environment and situation, and until I went through recovery, I had no idea why I was the way I was. It took over a year for me to pinpoint where some of my behaviors originated, and it was from there where I was able to start making changes.

Homosexuality

If you're reading this and you're LGBTQ, where can you begin looking for answers? Maybe start with your childhood, like I did: What role did your parents play? Grandparents? Extended family? Who was around? Who shouldn't have been around? What were you exposed to? Who were you hanging around with? Counseling is a great place, too, to talk and start looking at your life through a different lens.

Now, I don't want you to read this and feel like you're inherently wrong and hopeless. In fact, I want you to feel full of hope, that God made you to thrive, has an amazing plan for you, and that you can still prosper and be who you were created to be (Joshua 1:8)!

I went through a recovery program with a gay gentleman who had HIV. Through recovery, he discovered a lot about himself. Two years after I met him, he got married to a woman and is still attending recovery meetings and sharing his story of complete transformation.

However, I don't want you to read this and think I'm sitting here typing, "They choose to be gay." I don't think it's that obvious. Now, do some people willingly make that choice? Maybe. However, for many, it may not seem like a choice because it never was. Back to using my survival mechanisms, I didn't necessarily choose them, they were just part of who I was because of being born into a sinful world. Granted, I took responsibility for the choices I made (many painful decisions that hurt others), but I didn't know any better until I sat down with my counselor and started talking through things. Some of my discoveries were hard; I was manipulative, condescending, untrusting, and full of fear because of the house I grew up in. It pained me, but I also understood so much more. It's through understanding and hard work where change can happen.

Understanding being gay isn't always a choice, so what then? Each of us—daily—has the opportunity to sin: we could hold up a bank, murder a spouse, sleep around, and countless others. While opportunity is there for a multitude of sins, they don't become sins until we take next steps to act on them, whether physically or mentally. If homosexuality is a struggle for you, there are absolutely steps you can take: you can remain abstinent, change who you hang around with, stay single, change your thoughts instead of weighing on them, and more. A trusted Christian counselor or pastor can help you take tangible next steps.

For all of us, we want to be happy. We think we deserve to be happy. When we're not happy, we try to find what will make us happy. Growing up, success was what made me happy. It was short-lived. After every success, I would immediately jump back at it and start working towards my next success—a never-ending hamster wheel. For you, what do you think will make you happy? Alcohol? Drugs? Being accepted by someone of the same sex? Dressing like the opposite sex? Making up your own sex?

Through recovery, I came to learn that longing—*that desire to be happy*—would never be fulfilled on my own. It just wouldn't. I would burn out so fast trying to fill that void. The only way I could fill that void permanently was with God (Philippians 4:19).

I went through therapy, counseling, and various recovery groups, undoing decades of "success is happiness" and changing it to "God is happiness." Without God, there is no lasting happiness. You might be happy with the person you're with, or the actions you take, but it won't last, because people make mistakes and actions run their course like a burnt match.

It's a vicious cycle, isn't it? There is no happiness without God, but if you're gay, you might believe God hates you, so you stay as far away from God as possible, thus never being truly happy. I'm here to tell you *God doesn't hate you*; He loves you more than you know (Psalm 36:5–7). He might hate the sin, but you're more than your sins. Even when I was pursuing my own wants and needs, God still loved me. He never turned His back on me. And He still loves you, too.

I know this might be a lot to take in, but as you digest this content, know this: know you're loved and cared for, know I'm praying for you, and know *God loves you*.

> But God demonstrates His own love for us in this: While we were still sinners, Christ died for us. (Romans 5:8)

Gay Marriage

The Old Testament

- Genesis 2:24–25: "For this reason a man will leave his father and mother and be united to his wife, and they will become one flesh. The man and his wife were both naked, and they felt no shame."
- Deuteronomy 24:5: "If a man has recently married, he must not be sent to war or have any other duty laid on him. For one year he is to be free to stay at home and bring happiness to the wife he has married."
- Proverbs 18:22: "He who finds a wife finds what is good and receives favor from the Lord."
- Proverbs 19:14: "Houses and wealth are inherited from parents, but a prudent wife is from the Lord."
- Isaiah 62:5: "As a young man marries a maiden, so will your sons marry you; as a bridegroom rejoices over his bride, so will your God rejoice over you."

The New Testament

- Matthew 19:4–5: "'Haven't you read,' He replied, 'that at the beginning the Creator made them male and female,' and said,

'For this reason a man will leave his father and mother and be united to his wife, and the two will become one flesh?' So they are no longer two, but one. Therefore what God has joined together, let man not separate."

- Ephesians 5:28: "In the same way, husbands ought to love their wives as their own bodies."
- Colossians 3:18–19: "Wives, submit to your husbands, as is fitting in the Lord. Husbands, love your wives and do not be harsh with them."
- 1 Peter 3:7: "Husbands, in the same way be considerate as you live with your wives, and treat them with respect."

See also in its entirety Ephesians 5:22–33

Throughout His Word, God describes marriage as a relationship between a man and a woman, and that's how He designed it to be: between a husband and wife.

My wife and I married on November 23, 2019. Who would have predicted a few months later the world would be shut down by an international virus? Our first year of marriage was a challenge. My wife worked with Covid patients at her job while I worked at home, before being ultimately furloughed. I was able to collect unemployment, but the bills piled up and our emergency funds depleted to near-nothing. Throw all that on top of being married and adjusting to living together and you have yourself a ticking time bomb. However, by continually turning and remembering God's grace, we came out of "lockdown" closer together.

Before we got married, we spent a lot of time in joint counseling, making sure we were as ready as we could be for what the marriage road could hold. We went into marriage with our eyes open and knew it would be hard work. Keeping that in mind, both our counselor and our pastor shared with us God's design for marriage:

God created marriage as a reflection of how He loves His Church. The Church (capital "C") is His bride (Ephesians 5:28–29). Maybe most important in this relationship is how He loves His Church; although we make mistakes, doubt Him, and more,

Gay Marriage

He continues to love us unconditionally. In turn, that's how we're supposed to love our spouses; even though our spouses make mistakes, upset us, and get on our nerves, we're supposed to continually love them and show mercy, like God does for us (see previously referenced verses Ephesians 5:28, Colossians 3:18–19, and 1 Peter 3:7).

Throughout scripture, marriage is plainly defined as a relationship between a man and woman; even God describes Himself as the bridegroom and the Church as His bride (John 3:29). There is not one mention *in all of scripture* of a same-sex marriage.

God created men and women differently (despite what society is saying today). Men and women are unique and bring various personalities, traits, and roles to a marriage; they each have a separate role to play.

Marriage was not designed to have two males or two females; that upsets the balance and doesn't accomplish what God envisioned marriage to be. Men and women play specific roles in a marriage, and maybe even more so when kids enter the picture.

Kids need a strong mom *and* a strong dad. The percentage of children getting involved in drugs/alcohol, crime, and divorce catapult when they come from a home that's not a sound representation of the traditional nuclear family; there's not a coincidence between that fact and the fact God made marriage to be what it is. God wants what is best for us! He wants us to be successful in our relationships, He wants our kids to thrive, and He wants us to demonstrate His love for the world to see (Matthew 5:14–16), and how can we do that? By respecting His design and committing to heterosexual marriage.

Let's take this a step further: American society currently says gay marriage is legal, but as far as God is concerned, there is no such thing as gay marriage. As an institution, gay marriage is completely conceived by man, completely executed by man, and completely absent of God. Gay marriage is not a part of God's plan, no matter what society says is "okay."

Like I touched on in the previous chapter, for a lot of us, we're searching for whatever will fill that God-sized hole in our lives:

drugs, alcohol, sex—whatever. However, the high will run out and the God-sized hole will remain. Maybe you're thinking gay marriage will fill that void of loneliness or unacceptance. First hand, from my brief marriage experience, I know marriage doesn't fill any holes. Marriage is work and it takes a conscious decision every day to pursue your partner. There isn't a way for marriage to fill a hole; in time, without God, marriage will only cause more of a rift.

You might be thinking, "Haven't the number of gay marriages and people in the LGBTQ community skyrocketed in recent years? Isn't that a sign God's wrong? Why would He have created so many people 'wrong?'"

To further comment on what I stated in the previous chapter, I believe gay marriage is the result of outside circumstances, not internal ones. Let's press on this: if cocaine was legal and more available, how many more people would partake? What if prostitution was legal? What about pedophilia? How many of us get caught up in sin simply because society says it's *acceptable*, examples being pornography and alcoholism? Without any boundaries and a line that is continually moving, without being diligent to God and the Bible, in a few years time you'll see the legalization of pedophilia, cocaine and harder drugs, and worse. And that's a shocking guarantee.

It is our job as Christians to speak the truth of the Bible and make sure everyone knows it (James 5:19-20). How many people honestly don't know homosexuality or gay marriage is a sin? I recently searched online and found churches *in support* of homosexuality and gay marriage! Even churches are falling victim to societal agendas.

Without the Bible, we're so lost. We can't abandon or twist God's Word to fit in with our society. In fact, it should be the complete opposite: In a perfect Christ-like society, society would form around Biblical truths and not the other way around.

I know how hard it can be to change and listen to what God is saying. In my previous work, *A Voice from the Valley*, I explain how I was addicted to myself and what I wanted and how God was sitting on the sidelines. It took over a year of therapy, counseling, group sessions, and other work to get to a point where I could finally begin to surrender my desires before God and live a life for Him. It takes work, commitment, and a downright desire to want to change.

But why? Why did I *have* to change and surrender my desires for God's? *Because He wants what's best for me!* And He wants what's best for you, too. He doesn't put His truths in the Bible to hurt us, burn us, or make us feel unloved. Not at all. He has standards for us to live by because He wants us to live our best lives. It says in Galatians 5:19–24:

> The acts of the sinful nature are obvious: sexual immorality, impurity and debauchery; idolatry and witchcraft; hatred, discord, jealousy, fits of rage, selfish ambition, dissensions, factions and envy; drunkenness, orgies, and the like. I warn you, as I did before, that those who live like this will not inherit the kingdom of God.
>
> But the fruit of the Spirit is love, joy, peace, patience, kindness, goodness, faithfulness, gentleness and self-control. Against such things there is no law. Those who belong to Christ Jesus have crucified the sinful nature with its passion and desires.

God wants us to find pure happiness in Him. He wants to be what fills our God-sized holes. We need to surrender our wants and desires before Him and live what His Word says.

> "For I know the plans I have for you," declares the Lord, "plans to prosper you and not to harm you, plans to give you hope and a future." (Jeremiah 29:11)

Abortion

The Old Testament

- Exodus 20:13: "You shall not murder."
- Job 31:15: "Did not He who made me in the womb make them? Did not the same One form us both within our mothers?"
- Psalm 139:13–16a: "For You created my inmost being; You knit me together in my mother's womb. I praise You because I am fearfully and wonderfully made; Your works are wonderful, I know that full well. My frame was not hidden from You when I was made in the secret place. When I was woven together in the depths of the earth, Your eyes saw my unformed body."
- Jeremiah 1:5a: "Before I formed you in the womb I knew you, before you were born I set you apart."

The New Testament

- Matthew 19:14: "Jesus said, 'Let the little children come to me, and do not hinder them, for the kingdom of heaven belongs to such as these.'"
- Matthew 19:18b: "Jesus replied, 'Do not murder.'"

- Romans 12:1: "Therefore I urge you, brothers, in view of God's mercy, to offer your bodies as living sacrifices, holy and pleasing to God—this is your spiritual act of worship."
- 1 Corinthians 3:16–17: "Don't you know that you yourselves are God's temple and that God's Spirit lives in you? If anyone destroys God's temple, God will destroy him; for God's temple is sacred, and you are that temple."

Let me make this crystal clear: God does not approve of abortion; abortion is a sin aligned with murder.

Human beings are beautifully and wonderfully made *by Him*. Even before we were in our mother's wombs, He crafted, designed, and put the beauty of Himself in us.

In Isaiah 45:9, it says, "Does the clay say to the potter, 'What are you making?'" Abortion is taking the beautiful pot God created, lifting it above our heads, then smashing it against the ground.

But what about, "My body, my choice?" That's what we're told in society, right? That's what we hear: *My body, my choice*. Well, there is a choice. The choice is not to have sex in the first place. The choice is to wait until marriage, when you're financially stable, and when you're both ready for the lifetime commitment. Life is God's choice, not ours.

In the media, we see "Christian" politicians coming out and saying abortion is acceptable and that they support it. I don't care if you're red, blue, or green—the Bible is straightforward: Abortion is against God's law.

I hope you're ready to get real, because here we go: Abortion is murder. By aborting an unborn child, you are taking a living being, created by God (see previously referenced verses Job 31:15, Psalm 139:13, and Jeremiah 1:5a), and destroying it. That's murder.

And as important as all that is, here's another piece: The church is failing *miserably* when it comes to discussing abortion.

Although some churches are outspoken on their opposition of abortion, some of the largest ones keep their mouths shut. There is such a wishy-washy atmosphere inside some of the largest churches in America. I worked at a mega church (one of the largest in the U.S.), and at one point, I was discussing with my wife about buying a shirt that simply said *Pro-Life* and wearing it to work. We both decided, however, the shirt might be too controversial for where I worked. Isn't that insane, to where wearing a pro-life shirt at church would be deemed controversial? Pro-life isn't a political statement; it's a Biblical one.

I wonder what Jesus would say if He was asked about abortion? I don't want to put words in His mouth, but we're told the story of how He invited the little children to come to Him. His disciples wanted to keep the children away because (in their eyes) Jesus was too busy and too important to be bothered by them, but He stopped the disciples and said, "Heaven belongs to them" (Matthew 19:13-15).

Children and babies are innocent and need protecting. Shame on us and political figures who have passed bills to *fund* the murdering of God's creation. We're snuffing out amazing futures before their light is ever seen. What if God had created the person who was going to put an end to cancer, but before they ever could, they were aborted and destroyed? Sit with that for a moment.

I worked with a woman who was told to get an abortion. Late in her pregnancy, at a doctor's visit, they couldn't find the heartbeat of the child. On top of that, the baby had grown with several deformities. This woman—a strong woman of faith—said "no." She gave birth anyway to the lifeless and deformed baby.

I share that story because life isn't always easy; following what the Bible says *is not easy*, nor is it popular or non-confrontational. Only the strongest of us have the capability to make some of life's hardest decisions and disregard what politicians, the mob, or doctors say. At times, it's hard being a Christian, and it comes with pain, heartache, and persecution.

I know the world is saying one thing here and God is saying the complete opposite. Not only that, the world is encouraging premarital sex (which we'll discuss more later) which can only lead to more problems and brokenness. Again, following God's Word is not easy, but Jesus led by example: He came to earth and lived sinless among men. He knows our pains, struggles, and temptations,

ABORTION

and He's always there to listen to our open hearts when we cry out to Him (Psalm 145:18-19).

"Okay, Tim, but what about rape? What about birth-defects? What about risk to the mother? Then what?" In life, there are absolutely circumstances not brought on by the mother where doctors suggest abortion; so, where does that leave us? The Bible doesn't go deep into every circumstance we might come up against, but I would enter the situation with prayer, discernment, Christian counseling, and a consultation with a Christian doctor. However, all I can point to is what the Bible says, and what the Bible says is that God made that child. Does that mean the mother should have the child, even if it could put her life in danger? I don't know if I'm the one to answer that question, but what an act of love, the mother laying down her life for her child (John 15:13).

And if you're in a circumstance where abortion seems like the best option to you, know there are other options. There are plenty of parents out there who can't have kids of their own who are ready to adopt.

I can't imagine coming into this section having had an abortion in your own personal history. I want you to know Jesus loves you (1 John 4:15-16) and He died for you out of love. Accept His mercy and grace, then learn, change, and educate.

While writing this, my wife and I are expecting our first child; Natalie is twenty weeks along with our daughter. We had an ultrasound last week and it was my first time seeing and hearing my baby. I heard the rhythmic *whooshing* of her heartbeat. I saw her fingers and toes flexing, her face wincing, and her head bobbing; I actually saw her little heart pumping. Through a special lens, I was even able to see the charges going through her brain and the blood flowing through her veins. As I stared at the black and white monitor, looking at the outline of my daughter, I felt a connection. She's my daughter. And I'm proud of her. And I *love* her. Watching and hearing her, I thought of how amazing our God is, and that there was no doubt in my mind my daughter is a miracle—a living miracle. Just like every child. Those born and unborn.

The Most Offensive Book Ever Written

God loves His children. It's our responsibility now to educate others on what the Bible says, no matter your sex, race, or political affiliation, because more than anything else, we're Christians. Before anything else (before politics, family beliefs handed down, college lectures, or what we're pressured into following), the Bible and God's Word needs to be our primary resource when it comes to *any* of these topics, and what the Bible says goes. Period. Whether popular or not.

> Your Word is a lamp to my feet and a light for my path.
> (Psalm 119:105)

Drinking

The Old Testament

- Proverbs 20:1: "Wine is a mocker and beer a brawler; whoever is led astray by them is not wise."
- Proverbs 23:20–21: "Do not join those who drink too much wine or gorge themselves on meat, for drunkards and gluttons become poor, and drowsiness clothes them in rags."
- Isaiah 5:11: "Woe to those who rise early in the morning to run after their drinks, who stay up late at night till they were inflamed with wine."
- Habakkuk 2:15a: "Woe to him who gives drink to his neighbors, pouring it from the wineskin till they are drunk."

The New Testament

- Mark 14:23–25: "Then He took the cup, gave thanks and offered it to them, and they all drank from it. 'This is My blood of the covenant, which is poured out for many,' He said to them. 'I tell you the truth, I will not drink again of the fruit of the vine until that day when I drink it anew in the kingdom of God.'"

- Luke 21:34: "Be careful, or your hearts will be weighed down with dissipation, drunkenness and the anxieties of life, and that day will close on you unexpectedly like a trap."

- Romans 13:13–14: "Let us behave decently, as in the daytime, not in orgies and drunkenness, not in sexual immorality and debauchery, not in dissension and jealousy. Rather, clothe yourselves with the Lord Jesus Christ, and do not think about how to gratify the desires of the sinful nature."

- 1 Corinthians 6:10: "Nor thieves nor the greedy nor drunkards nor slanderers nor swindlers will inherit the kingdom of God."

- Galatians 5:19–21: "The acts of the sinful nature are obvious: sexual immorality, impurity and debauchery; idolatry and witchcraft; hatred, discord, jealousy, fits of rage, selfish ambition, dissensions, factions and envy; drunkenness, orgies, and the like. I warn you, as I did before, that those who live like this will not inherit the kingdom of God."

Alright, friends, let's talk about something light and fun—like drinking!

Sarcasm.

Looking at what the Bible says, in short: drinking is not a sin, but getting drunk is, and there is certainly a distinction.

I feel like this is pretty obvious. Going out and partying, or staying in and getting drunk, that seems bad, right? It *seems* like something we could all get behind and say is wrong and move onto the next topic, but unfortunately, it's really not. So many of us continually drop the ball here. The Bible plainly says drunkenness is a sin.

Hey Christians, did you all hear that? *Getting drunk is a sin!* Seems like a lot of us have forgotten . . .

I know Christians that have been/are alcoholics, but I also know Christians that go out and casually drink, having a single martini with a friend, or a glass of wine. So what's the distinction? There is not a problem with having a drink or two; in the Bible, even Jesus drank wine, and having a pint with family and friends is

DRINKING

a great way to commune and fellowship and has been for thousands of years. However, there is a clear line to avoid: getting drunk.

"Tim, are you really saying if I go out and get tipsy at a wedding, or have one too many at a concert, or get silly at a family party—that's a sin?!" Here's another distinction: I'm not saying that; *God is* (as stated in the introduction of this work, read 2 Timothy 3:16).

Christians, we're called to a higher standard. I know what goes on in high schools, colleges, and homes across America; so many people partying on the weekends (or more unhealthily during the week) and we're told that's normal, and if we don't do that we're "goody-goodies" or "Jesus freaks" (let's bring that term back!).

Again, I don't see there being anything wrong with having a beer or a glass of wine (there are even some medical studies out saying there are health benefits to alcohol in limited moderation), but getting drunk—even once—that's a sin.

As followers of Christ, we need to start leading here. At weddings, be the DD. At family parties, show your kids and cousins you don't have to get plastered to have a good time. When you go out to bars with friends, spread out your drinks. Looking at the Bible, I don't see going to bars or breweries as sins; I see the act of drinking until drunk as a sin.

I was drawn to this topic because, Christians, we're failing bad here! I've seen Christians get drunk and make fools out of themselves and not think twice about it. Not only is getting drunk bad for your health, but from the perspective of the world, what do they think? "Isn't that so-and-so, *that Christian*?" People should know you're a Christian by your lifestyle (Matthew 5:16). God calls us to be different, and that we're not to conform to the pattern of this world (Romans 12:2).

This world loves alcohol, I'm a Budweiser man myself, but we need to sacrifice drunkenness and surrender to God's will.

I know what some of you are thinking: "There goes God again, being a buzzkill" (pun), but you're stopping short. Think for a moment on the *why*. Why does God want you to refrain from drunkenness?

God loves you. He fights for you. He's passionate about you. Would a God who truly loves you pull something from you that makes you happy if it was *truly* good for you in the long run? The answer is no (Romans 8:28).

Being drunk never leads to good decisions or faithful Christianity. What it leads to is broken homes, car wrecks, unfaithfulness, ridiculous arguments, embarrassment, generational trauma, and the possibility of dancing with a lampshade on your head. If you're keeping up with me—those are all bad.

God doesn't say avoid drunkenness because He doesn't want you to enjoy the life He's given you; He says to avoid drunkenness to steer clear of the unnecessary pain that goes with it.

Friends, drunkenness is something I grew up around. It's a heartbreaking sickness that robs, cheats, and steals.

"Okay, that's bad—obviously—but what about getting drunk occasionally? I'm not an alcoholic, but what about getting drunk once a week, or once a month even? Does God really care about that?"

Yeah, He does. Anytime you're drunk, you're leaving yourself completely open to an attack from the enemy (1 Peter 5:8). When you're in your sane mind, you have a team in the firehouse ready to put out the fire. When you're drunk—that team goes home. You're leaving all the decision making to your half-a-mind, making yourself prone to poor decision making. I think we've all heard extremely hurtful and revealing truths from those who've spoken while drunk.

God is not the bad guy here. He has laws in place to protect us from ourselves and from the Devil. God wants us to flourish; He wants us to embrace the fruits of the Spirit and thrive (Galatians 5:22–23).

> Can a man scoop fire into his lap without his clothes being burned? Can a man walk on hot coals without his feet being scorched? (Proverbs 6:27–28)

Divorce

The Old Testament

- Genesis 2:24: "For this reason a man will leave his father and mother and be united to his wife, and they will become one flesh."
- Jeremiah 3:1: "'If a man divorces his wife and she leaves him and marries another man, should he return to her again? Would not the land be completely defiled?'"
- Malachi 2:15–16: "Has not the Lord made them one? In flesh and spirit they are His. And why one? Because He was seeking godly offspring. So guard yourself in your spirit, and do not break faith with the wife of your youth. 'I hate divorce,' says the Lord God of Israel."

The New Testament

- Matthew 5:31–32: "It has been said, 'Anyone who divorces his wife must give her a certificate of divorce.' But I tell you that anyone who divorces his wife, except for marital unfaithfulness, causes her to become an adulteress, and anyone who marries the divorced woman commits adultery."
- Mark 10:6–12: "But at the beginning of creation God 'made them male and female.' 'For this reason a man will leave his

father and mother and be united to his wife, and the two will become one flesh.' So they are no longer two, but one. Therefore what God has joined together, let man not separate.' When they were in the house again, the disciples asked Jesus about this. He answered, 'Anyone who divorces his wife and marries another woman commits adultery against her. And is she divorces her husband and marries another man, she commits adultery.'"

- 1 Corinthians 7:10b–11: "A wife must not separate from her husband. But if she does, she must remain unmarried or else be reconciled to her husband. And a husband must not divorce his wife."

- 1 Corinthians 7:39: "A woman is bound to her husband as long as he lives. But if her husband dies, she is free to marry anyone she wishes, but he must belong to the Lord."

- Ephesians 5:33: "Each one of you also must love his wife as he loves himself, and the wife must respect her husband."

God's words: *I hate divorce.*

I have three people close to me who have gone through divorce. It's bitter, frustrating, and assaults a person's self-esteem. Psychiatrists even equate the emotional toll of divorce to that of a death.

God wasn't being cute when he said, "the two will become one flesh." I believe He meant it literally: He created marriage to be a *complete* partnership between two people—two acting as one, building off each other, being twice the person they would be by themselves.

You sometimes see this illustration at weddings, where the bride and groom have bottles of sand in their favorite colors, and then they mix their sands together into one bottle. What a great representation of God's view of marriage: the two becoming one. Where would one flesh pull away from the other? How long would it take to place each grain of sand back into its original bottle?

God hates divorce because it's all but impossible in His eyes; how do you separate a single, unified flesh back into two parts?

DIVORCE

The effects of divorce ripple through the family. Kids lose stability and unity: they're more likely to develop a mental disorder, have a health issue, struggle in school, and ultimately get divorced themselves. God created family to be just that—a family. Moms and dads are supposed to be there to support their kids—*together*. When dad fails, mom is there. When mom fails, dad is there. Mom and dad are a unit—a team—a single mechanism driving the household. Take an entire half of that away and the end result can be devastating.

Not only on kids, either. Couples who've gone through divorce say it's one of the most heart-wrenching situations a person can go through in their lives. Being in a divorce, your world gets completely upended and you get dragged back to the starting line. Secrets are out, family conflicts rage, and trust is completely shattered, maybe never to be completely restored.

But before we move further, let's cover something pivotal: through the words of Jesus, I understand divorce being *acceptable* if there was/is unfaithfulness by a spouse. I personally can't imagine having an unfaithful spouse. I don't know what feelings I would have; I'm sure "heartbreaking" is a word that does zero justice. But Jesus saw the excruciating pain in unfaithfulness and said it's acceptable as grounds for divorce (see previously referenced verses Matthew 5:31–32).

"But what about abuse—physical, mental, or verbal? What about addiction? Aren't those all good reasons to get a divorce, too?" Friends, this is where it gets hard. From what I've read and understand, the Bible states unfaithfulness as the only grounds for divorce.

I can't begin to comprehend dealing with abuse or addiction in a marriage. You deserve love, tenderness, and respect, and if you're not receiving those, someone is *not* holding up their end of the bargain; they are failing both you and your family. And quite frankly, from a very human perspective, they probably don't deserve your love, but that's me talking, not God. Jesus teaches us—through marriage—to love the unlovable like He loves us (Ephesians 5:1–2).

If you're in a situation of abuse, I'd urge you to talk with a Christian counselor and a pastor for further guidance and next steps—they'll help you find recovery options, safety, and mental health resources. Maybe there's an option to separate while someone heals, without permanent divorce. I don't know. But no matter what, please continue to believe in miracles (Deuteronomy 10:21), please continue to believe in redemption, and please continue to believe God can heal even the most broken of hearts. It's never too late; our God is Jehovah Rapha (the Lord who heals). Know I'm praying for you and your situation. May the Lord of all—who sees all—guide you and may you hear His voice.

> Two are better than one, because they have a good return for their work: If one falls down, his friend can help him up. But pity the man who falls and has no one to help him up! Also, if two lie down together, they will keep warm. But how can one keep warm alone? Though one may be overpowered, two can defend themselves. A cord of three strands is not quickly broken. (Ecclesiastes 4:9–12)

Now, honestly, I don't think any of us go into marriage hoping we'll get divorced. Instead, we go into marriage with the biggest hopes and grandest dreams, wanting to live that fairytale life with a happy ending. But it doesn't take long for us to realize marriage isn't a fairytale.

When God talks about divorce, He makes it abundantly clear marriage isn't a joke, and anyone considering marriage should understand staying married isn't a choice—it's a bond no man should separate.

If you go into marriage with the mindset, "Well, I'll have a way out if things get hard," you know what's going to happen? You'll fold when things get hard. However, if you go into marriage with the mindset, "No matter what happens, that other person is my spouse and we've sworn an oath before God," you're going to find ways to fight together and overcome life's toughest obstacles.

Marriage has become a ridiculous amusement in our culture. Celebrities get married for weeks before they divorce, and 50%

Divorce

of marriages end in divorce, and that percentage is just as high in our churches.

So before my wife and I got married, our pastor made sure we knew what we were getting into: it's going to get hard and there's going to be trials, so make sure you have a foundation of grace in Jesus to make it through.

Marriage is supposed to be a beautiful image of how Jesus loves His people, constantly forgiving them and showing them love when they don't deserve it. How many of us actually do that in our own marriages, though? Instead, we hang onto hurts, build resentment, and let bitterness fester.

Husbands, we're supposed to love our wives, and wives, you're supposed to respect us. Marriages immediately begin to fall apart when the balance of love and respect tips one way over the other. Love and respect too often become dependent on action, and then they're taken away due to inaction. But that's not how Jesus loves. Jesus loves us while we're still sinners. We need to be quick to forgive and slow to speak (James 1:19–22). We need to be gentle with our spouses, not covered in thorns when we embrace.

God laid down the severity of divorce. He didn't mince words. And why? *Because we're not supposed to rush into marriage!* Seriously. What's the rush? Again, who cares what society says: "You should be married by this age and have kids by that age." No. You know what, they don't get to decide. You do. Don't get married until you're *100% certain* of your spouse.

On top of that, go into marriage with your eyes open. Have the tough conversations before the "I dos" start flying. Talk about kids, politics, church, family roles, who's working, who's not, where you're going to live, the relationships you'll keep, what your expectations are on the weekends, etc. Don't get married and then realize one of you wants kids and the other doesn't. That's not going into marriage well. Take the time. Ask the questions. Seek counsel. God wants a marriage that will glorify and honor Him, not one that will fall apart at the first sign of conflict.

Speaking of conflict, marriage doesn't fix your relationship problems; it amplifies them. If someone has an addiction but says they'll fix it when you're married, guess what—don't bet on it. Marriage is stressful and there are temptations around every corner. You need to have your head right going into it. If you struggle with communication, it will only get worse in marriage. If there's jealousy, lack of trust, or unfaithfulness before marriage, odds are those traits will continue into marriage and shoot up like weeds. Do the hard work on the front end to go into marriage well!

Marriage is sacred and God loves it. He loves seeing two people honor, respect, and love each other *in His name*. It's nothing that should be rushed into. It should be a decision you weigh on heavily. And listen to your heart; if you're having true doubts backed up by evidence, take your time.

Get married *once*; let that first person be your forever. And both agree there's no turning back—for better or worse, richer or poorer, in sickness and health, never to be separated.

Love never fails. (1 Corinthians 13:8a)

The Death Penalty

The Old Testament

- Genesis 9:5b–6: "And from each man, too, I will demand an accounting for the life of his fellow man. 'Whoever sheds the blood of man, by man shall his blood be shed; for in the image of God has God made man.'"
- Exodus 21:12: "Anyone who strikes a man and kills him shall surely be put to death."
- Numbers 35:30–31: "Anyone who kills a person is to be put to death as a murderer only on the testimony of witnesses. But no one is to be put to death on the testimony of only one witness. Do not accept a ransom for the life of a murderer, who deserves to die. He must surely be put to death."

The New Testament

- Matthew 5:38–41: "You have heard that it was said, 'Eye for eye, and tooth for tooth.' But I tell you, do not resist an evil person. If someone strikes you on the right cheek, turn to him the other also. And if someone wants to sue you and take your tunic, let him have your cloak as well. If someone forces you to go one mile, go with him two miles."

- Matthew 5:43–44: "You have heard that it was said, 'Love your neighbor and hate your enemy.' But I tell you: Love your enemies and pray for those who persecute you."
- Romans 4:25: "He was delivered over to death for our sins and was raised to life for our justification."
- James 4:12: "There is only one Lawgiver and Judge, the one who is able to save and destroy. But you—who are you to judge your neighbor?"
- 1 John 3:15: "Anyone who hates his brother is a murderer, and you know that no murderer has eternal life in him."

In our human hearts, we desire death as punishment for the most horrid of crimes, but I don't see the New Testament giving us permission to do that.

This is the first topic we've tackled where there is a polar opposite between what the Old and New Testaments say.

It's pretty obvious capital punishment was okay in the Old Testament; I see it used as a tactic by God to keep His people in line with the laws He had handed down. His people (the Israelites) were chosen and special (Deuteronomy 7:6); He wanted them to act differently than other tribes and people. Several times in the Pentateuch, we see the penalty of a crime resulting in justifiable death, from murder to lewd sexual acts. Capital punishment was allowed under God's law.

However, Jesus teaches us something different in the New Testament. He brings up the Law given to Moses and the Israelites and says, "You have heard that it was said, 'Eye for eye, and tooth for tooth.' But I tell you, do not resist an evil person. If someone strikes you on the right cheek, turn to him the other also" (Matthew 5:38–39). Although He is not specifically addressing murder here, He is addressing the Law, and because He's addressing the Law, I believe it's fair to infer He's addressing the penalty of the Law as well.

Before just a few months ago, I was a firm believer in the death penalty. It seemed right to me. I didn't have much Biblical

THE DEATH PENALTY

knowledge on the issue, but it *felt* right: If you kill someone, you should be killed.

When I think about murderers and the pain they've inflicted on the friends and families left behind, my heart bleeds, then grows cold. Timothy McVeigh. James Holmes. Dzhokhar Tsarnaev. Osama Bin Laden. And so many others. They took lives. They took away everything someone could have been. And you want to know something? Let me be honest: In my human heart, there is a part that wants to hate them—*I* want to hate them. I want to see them punished, and in my heart, some of them already got what they deserved.

In doing that, though, by hating them, according to Jesus' words, I'm just as guilty as they are.

Jesus said, "You have heard that it was said to the people long ago, 'You shall not murder, and anyone who murders will be subject to judgment.' But I tell you that anyone who is angry with a brother or sister will be subject to judgment" (Matthew 5:21–22a).

Through Jesus, as Christians, we are now held to a higher standard.

Jesus reminds us we're all sinners. He put murder and hate on the same level. He more or less said, "Stop pointing a finger at them. *You are them.* You deserve to die, too . . . but I paid your price."

Because of that, I can't believe in punishing sin with death. I don't believe that's our call. Isaiah 53:6 says, "We all, like sheep, have gone astray, each of us has turned to our own way; and the Lord has laid on Him the iniquity of us all."

But let me make a critical distinction: should a murderer still be *punished* by human laws? Yes! Should they be in prison and removed from society? Yes. Actions have consequences. I don't believe prison is a sin. Removing a threat in the safety of others isn't wrong. But all of that being stated, I don't believe a person should pay for their wrongs with their own life, even as much as my human heart might want them to. Jesus already paid for their wrongs with *His* life.

In fact, we all need a refresher course in truly believing Jesus is the God of miracles. He can change hearts. He can save and restore. Paul—writer of the majority of the New Testament—before becoming a Christian, gave permission to murder Christians! But God took him and transformed him. When we throw someone under the penalty of death, we're taking away what God *can do* inside that person. We, too, are taking away anything they could ever be.

"But that person deserves to be punished!" And they will be. They'll spend time in prison (maybe even the rest of their lives), completely removed from society and the joys you and I have access to on a daily basis—family, friends, and activities, but more important is this: God is a God of justice. He is Adonai (The God who Rules). He will handle their judgment (2 Timothy 4:1). Those who were murdered or killed, God loved them more than we ever could; they were His. We can find peace in knowing God will be just and strike with punishment.

Now, some of this might seem a bit confusing, right? How can there be such a shift in tone from the Old Testament to the New Testament? Did God change His mind?

Absolutely not! In the Old Testament, God was doing everything He could to set His people up for success. He wanted them to be different than the rest of the tribes and countries. He wanted their reputation to proceed them, that they were His *chosen* people who had been set apart (Leviticus 20:24). In the Old Testament, too, sins were paid with blood. Sacrifices of animals paid the debt of sin, and in certain cases people paid for their sins with their own blood and lives. In the New Testament, though, Jesus took that place. He died for *all* sin. Now the only blood necessary to cover sins is His.

So, no, God never changed His mind—His plan remained the same: He knew and had planned that Jesus would come and pay for the sins of the world, and that whoever would believe in Him would not perish, but have everlasting life (John 3:16).

With Jesus came a change of the rules. Blood and sacrifice were no longer necessary; He paid the bill. And that's where the change comes between Testaments: death no longer needs to be repaid with death; Jesus died so we can forgive, love, and hope.

The Death Penalty

Yet, please don't hear me saying that as Christians we are commanded to give passes to murderers. I'm not saying that and I don't believe the Bible says that. God is a God of justice and He *will* judge. What I am saying, and what I believe the Bible and Jesus say, is that instead of repaying blood for blood, let's believe God can do miracles and work in that person's heart (Psalm 77:13-14). Who knows what good they can do through the rest of their lives? Who knows the people they can reach behind bars that we can't? Who knows what a single drop of mercy and compassion can do when it hits a calloused and misguided heart?

When we find ways to love like Jesus, we're not giving anyone a pass or approving any type of behavior; we're taking a step of faith and believing miracles can still be done.

> I will give you a new heart and put a new spirit in you; I will remove from you your heart of stone and give you a heart of flesh. (Ezekiel 36:26)

Heterosexual Marriage

The Old Testament

- Genesis 2:24–25: "For this reason a man will leave his father and mother and be united to his wife, and they will become one flesh. The man and his wife were both naked, and they felt no shame."
- Proverbs 19:14b: "A prudent wife is from the Lord."
- Isaiah 62:5: "As a young man marries a maiden, so will your sons marry you; as a bridegroom rejoices over his bride, so will your God rejoice over you."
- Jeremiah 29:6a: "Marry and have sons and daughters; find wives for your sons and give your daughters in marriage, so that they too may have sons and daughters."

The New Testament

- 1 Corinthians 6:14: "Do not be yoked with unbelievers. For what do righteousness and wickedness have in common? Or what fellowship can light have with darkness?"
- Ephesians 5:22–23: "Wives, submit to your husbands as to the Lord. For the husband is the head of the wife as Christ is the head of the Church, His body, of which He is the Savior."

Heterosexual Marriage

- Ephesians 5:25-27: Husbands, love your wives, just as Christ loved the Church and gave Himself up for her to make her holy, cleansing her by the washing with water through the Word, and to present her to Himself as a radiant Church, without stain or wrinkle or any other blemish, but holy and blameless."

- 1 Peter 3:1: "Wives, in the same way be submissive to your husbands so that, if any of them do not believe the Word, they may be won over without words by the behavior of their wives."

- 1 Peter 3:7: "Husbands, in the same way be considerate as you live with your wives, and treat them with respect as the weaker partner and as heirs with you of the gracious gift of life, so that nothing will hinder your prayers."

See also in their entirety Ephesians 5:22-33 and 1 Peter 3:1-7

Men and women were designed to have specific roles in a marriage and those roles are different from each other.

I can already sense a bunch of women racking their shotguns—don't run amok just yet!

First and foremost, using the Bible as our mirror, heterosexual marriage in modern society looks nothing like it should. Society has wives wielding all the power with husbands falling behind, living in their man caves, and not even being necessary. Kids and minors are now even making adult decisions that can alter their lives forever (especially when it comes to issues of sexuality and gender identity). Society is flailing and pushing for the disintegration of the family as God would have it.

Modern societal movements are also altering the shape of heterosexual marriage. As Christians, we absolutely believe in equality between men and women—we were all created equal, absolutely—but here is where modern movements have it wrong: Biblically speaking, women are not supposed to be the heads of the household. Men are.

"Wait, wait, wait. Husbands are supposed to rule over their wives? What is this—1952?"

Before we jump to any conclusions, let's read what the Bible actually says and understand it in context:

Paul writes, "For the husband is the head of the wife as Christ is the head of the Church" (Ephesians 5:23). I'm sure, for some of you, there are two different thoughts going: 1) Wives, you don't like the sound of that, the husbands being the head, and 2) Husbands, you like the sound of that, making yourselves up to be kings. Here is where women are going to start enjoying it, though, and men aren't . . .

Paul compares husbands to Christ leading the Church. Christ led by example. And how did He lead? By loving, serving, forgiving, and sacrificing. That's how husbands are supposed to be the head in a marriage.

Husbands, we're failing—*bad*. For a lot of us, we kind of like what society has been pushing. We like sitting back, taking a secondary role, and letting our wives run the show. It's easier, less stressful, and allows more time for beer, sports, and video games. Guys, I get it. I really do. It's nice to relax after working hard, but we're not called to a secondary role in marriage.

Beer, sports, and video games are fine, as long as they come secondary to being the head in a marriage and leading by example. Like Jesus, we're supposed to be serving our wives, loving them, being gentle with them, and sacrificing for them. For a lot of us husbands, we haven't come close to hitting that nail (some of us haven't even swung the hammer).

Now, wives, Paul also says, "Wives, submit to your husbands as to the Lord" (Ephesians 5:22). When was the last time you submitted to your husband?

I know, for a lot of you, your minds run to servanthood, right? Or "being seen and not heard." In those scenarios, the servant acts out of fear. However, if your husband is loving, serving, and honoring *you*, submission looks a lot different; submission looks like respect.

Heterosexual Marriage

Science tells us more than love, men cherish respect. As a man, we don't like being second-guessed, nagged, or belittled; we want to be submitted to out of respect and out of trust. When we say something and we're constantly second-guessed or nagged over and over, we don't feel respected, and when we don't feel respected we don't feel loved.

Society keeps telling us to push the envelope and knock down marriage stereotypes and for the woman to be dominant and for the man to be submissive. Men don't thrive when they're submissive. Men thrive most when there is a strong woman in their corner who is cheering for, encouraging, trusting, and respecting them.

In the same way, women don't thrive when they're not loved by their partner. Love shouldn't come just when they do their makeup, complete chores, make a meal, throw down a paycheck, or pick up the kids from school. Love in marriage should not be dependent on acts. Husbands, love should flow freely from us to our wives. They don't need to earn it from us; they should already have it.

My wife and I had our good friends from Texas over this past weekend. While out to dinner, we were talking Biblical gender roles (because who doesn't discuss that over pulled pork sandwiches), and our friend Sophie said, "What it comes down to is, for girls who are dating or engaged, they need to ask themselves if the man they're with is worth submitting to." Dang. What a question. Husbands are supposed to be respected, but women, before going into marriage, is your man worthy of your respect? Will he lead a Godly house? *Is he worthy of your submission*? If your answer is "no," you shouldn't be saying "I do."

But why did God designate marriage to be this way? Is it because He respects men and not women? Is it because women are inferior to men? Is it because men are winners and women are losers? No, no, and no. With this point in particular, the Bible is often taken out of context. As soon as society sees "wives, submit to your husbands," the clap back is usually that the Bible is misogynistic, outdated, and non-relevant. But the true "why" is never taken into consideration.

God is smarter than us and always has a specific plan in place. He designed marriage to look a particular way and for the members of a marriage to act a certain way. And why? Because He wants marriage to be successful.

Husbands and wives are put into their roles for ultimate love and respect reciprocity. Leading the household, men are respected. Aiding and serving the man, women are loved. And look at kids, too—kids need examples to follow; they need respected men and loved women in their lives. When families start to look nontraditional, structure and stability go out the window and feelings (instead of God's Law) begin to run the house. From there, kids get conflicting messages about gender roles, financial goals, and the importance of educational/personal targets.

God didn't design heterosexual marriage willy-nilly; He designed it in mind with husbands, wives, and children each playing specific roles.

So, let's take some time, do some further reading, and get our marriages back to looking like they should. Husbands, let's stand up, get involved, and lead our houses under God. Let's take responsibility. And let's love our wives. Cherish them. Sacrifice for and serve them. They are the only person in the world we've chosen to spend the rest of our lives with—let's act like it!

And wives, please respect and trust us. We are only as strong as you are. We need your honor and we need your help.

Families don't run on one parent; it takes two, and God designed it that way.

> Now as the Church submits to Christ, so also wives should submit to their husbands in everything. (Ephesians 5:24)

Pornography

The Old Testament

- Exodus 20:17b: "You shall not covet your neighbor's wife, or his manservant or maidservant."
- Numbers 15:39: "You will have these tassels to look at and so you will remember all the commands of the Lord, that you may obey them and not prostitute yourselves by going after the lusts of your own hearts and eyes."
- Proverbs 6:25: "Do not lust in your heart after her beauty or let her captivate you with her eyes."

The New Testament

- Matthew 5:28: "But I tell you that anyone who looks at a woman lustfully has already committed adultery with her in his heart."
- Romans 13:13–14: "Let us behave decently, as in the daytime, not in orgies and drunkenness, not in sexual immorality and debauchery, not in dissension and jealousy. Rather, clothe yourselves with the Lord Jesus Christ, and do not think about how to gratify the desires of the sinful nature."

- 1 Corinthians 6:18–19: "Flee from sexual immorality. All other sins a man commits are outside his body, but he who sins sexually sins against his own body. Do you not know that your body is a temple of the Holy Spirit, who is in you, whom you have received from God? You are not your own."

- 1 Thessalonians 4:3–5: "It is God's will that you should be sanctified: that you should avoid sexual immorality; that each of you should learn to control his own body in a way that is holy and honorable, not in passionate lust like the heathen, who do not know God."

- Titus 2:11–12: "For the grace of God that brings salvation has appeared to all men. It teaches us to say 'No' to ungodliness and worldly passions, and to live self-controlled, upright and godly lives in this present age."

No matter what society says is acceptable, the Bible says pornography *is not*. End of story. (*Note: in this case, I'm using lust and pornography as synonyms. Although the Bible does not speak "pornography" by name, pornography doesn't exist without lust*)

This topic couldn't be any more timely.

Our culture is hyper-sexualized (and that might even be an understatement). We're told being curious is okay, being sexual is okay (at whatever age, really, right? In the Chicago Public Schools, they're offering birth control to 5th graders!), and that pornography is okay.

First off, why is the Bible against pornography and in favor of self-control? For example, pornography taints expectations of future spouses; we'll expect our spouses to look a certain way, act a certain way, and be sexual in a certain way. We all know the feeling of expectations, whether expectations others have put on us or we have put on ourselves. Imagine your spouse walking into your marriage with specific sexual expectations for you to fulfill. How would you feel in that spot? Uneasy? Assigned? Unloved? In the marriage bed, you wouldn't be spending time with your spouse; you'd be fulfilling fantasies your partner has had in their head with others for however many years.

God designed marriage and sex to be pure, where both partners enter marriage as virgins so they can explore sex together. Pornography destroys that purity and zigzags through shortcuts.

Sex with your spouse is more than the act of sex; it's about love, emotional connection, and exploration. *Porn isn't that.* Porn is sex for simple gratification. There isn't an emotional connection. There's only lust.

And here's something else: Do you want your spouse to be like the people in those videos, magazines, and ads? Honestly now. I once heard a pastor talking about relationships, and he told a story of how he was in a bar and an attractive woman came in wearing a low-cut shirt and short skirt. He said, "Looking at her, I knew she could be a good time, but not a good wife."

We should all have high standards for our spouses. We should want them to enter marriage as pure as they can, without their minds being warped by the extremely unrealistic expectations found in porn. Whatever your expectations are, throw those out the door when you enter marriage, because your spouse has a say in what happens in the bedroom.

The Devil is focusing his armies on attacking marriages, because Christian marriages (when completely rooted in Christ) can overcome the toughest obstacles. Evil is coming for your marriage however he can, with a desire to fracture it, and if that means tempting you with porn so you hold unreal expectations with your spouse, which could lead to sexual frustration, which could lead to an addiction to porn or an affair, then so be it!

We don't need porn, no matter what society is trying to jam down our throats and tell us is good for us. God has challenged us to be different (Proverbs 1:15). He has given us the Bible, and the Bible is our guide on how to best succeed in our marriages. Let's listen to what it says!

"But is porn *really* that bad? Does it really have that high a cost?" Growing up, there was a fun Christian couple in my church that I volunteered with occasionally, but down the line their marriage ended because the husband was addicted to porn and would then ask his wife to be like the girls in the videos he watched. Porn can honestly mean your marriage. Whether you're a kid or an adult, don't get caught in the trap that's been placed for you. Kick it early. It's never going to lead to anything good. *Ever.*

Jesus pushes it further. Are you ready for this? He says, "Anyone who looks at a woman lustfully has already committed adultery with her in his heart" (Matthew 5:28). I find it interesting that He's talking to men here. Essentially, Jesus is saying, "If you're a married man and you check out and lust after that cute girl in line at the Burger King, that's the same as cheating on your wife." In Jesus' eyes, porn is the same as picking up a woman at a bar and having an affair.

I want to take the men aside for a moment here: Men, I know this is hard. Statistics show men are more interested in porn than women are. And why? When God created Eve for Adam, He created a woman that would fulfill Adam's physical desires. Women are created in a way where we're naturally drawn to them; we find women attractive, from their hair and curves to lack of beards, etc. Speaking from constant experience, I know it's hard to control lust, and not just porn, but lust in general.

There are beautiful girls everywhere: in advertisements, on the road, at work, but Jesus says not to lust. We need to do better here. It's human nature to notice the people around us, and that's fine, but pray for strength and self-control to combat that second look. Let's claw to keep our hearts pure, for God and for our spouses.

For those of us who are married, our bodies belong to our spouses. They don't belong to the people acting or posing. "But he/she does this, and looks this way, and my spouse won't—" No. Those people in porn are not the people you joined hands with and swore an oath before God with that nothing would come between the two of you.

And if you or your spouse are sexually frustrated, it's okay to ask for help and seek a Christian counselor. God wants us to enjoy sex! It's an intimate bond. It's okay to seek help for a better sex life just like you would for any other marital concern. You'll get a chance to listen to each other and hear each other's wants/needs. Maybe it's worth a shot?

I honestly don't care what society says. God says sexuality should be between you and your spouse and that's it. Single people, this applies to you, too. Outside of the marriage bed, there shouldn't be sexuality through movies, computer screens, social media posts, books, magazines, or anything else.

Christians, we're called to be better, so let's be better. We need to pray for self-control, be creative with finding ways to avoid lust (deleting social media, keeping a picture of our spouse by our computer screens, being open and honest with an accountability partner, counseling, or whatever else we have to do), and fight against the riptide of sexuality that is trying to take us out and drown us.

Satan wants to slaughter our relationships, whether in marriage or while we're still single. He's spilled enough blood. Let's not give him any more.

> For our struggle is not against flesh and blood, but against the rulers, against the authorities, against the powers of this dark world and against the spiritual forces of evil in the heavenly realms. (Ephesians 6:12)

Intermission

Welcome to intermission! A little The Offspring reference there.

I can't believe we've made it this far—just about halfway. I know it's been a lot and that it's been heavy, but we have some big topics coming up, too. So, before we jump back in, let's take a couple moments and breathe.

Breathe in. Breathe out. Breathe in. Breathe out.

Who who he. Who who he. Isn't that what pregnant women are supposed to do in labor? I don't know. Maybe. I should probably find that out; my wife is giving birth in a couple months! Feels like we're giving birth here . . . okay, after doing some further research, "who who he" is no longer taught. There's your tip for the day!

Anyone have a funny joke to share? How about this: What do you call a baby that won't sleep? Any guesses? *A baby!* I literally made that up just now.

Seriously, though, before we dive back in, let's re-center ourselves and remember why we're on this road of discovery together: We're not going over these topics to purposely aggravate anyone or to be "holier than thou;" we're going over these topics so we know the truth about what God wants for us and what He has planned for us.

Look at it this way: You don't jump into a game of soccer, start making up your own rules (like you can carry the ball and throw it in the goal), and then be mad at the referee once they penalize you. But that's exactly where we're at in society. God created life and

INTERMISSION

made clear what He desires for us. Who are we now to turn around and be upset with God that we don't like His way of playing?

God's plans for a holy way of life came long before ours. We're trying to change the game. We're saying it's not fair. We're saying it's sexist, racist, "old way of thinking," or boring. When, in fact, it's none of those things; we just want to play the game our own way and that's where the problem is—we want to be God. We want to make the world how we would have it and wasn't that exactly how Satan tempted Adam and Eve (Genesis 3:5)?

We want the world to be this all-inclusive place where no one is offended by anything and no one gets in trouble for anything and you can be anything you want to be (or anybody you want to be) whenever you want. You know what God says to all of that? He says "No." He says, "You don't get to make the rules. This is *My* world you're living in, and I created it for you, and I want you to thrive and succeed in it, but in order for you to do that, you have to read My Word, study it, and then apply it."

But that's too hard for a lot of us. We don't want rules or boundaries or guidelines. We want to do things our own way.

"Why can't we do things our way?" Well, it's led to mass cases of depression and anxiety on an epidemic scale, unprecedented numbers of suicides and divorces, and a generation for the first time in American history worse off than the one before it. And you know why? The more a generation takes its eyes out of the Bible, the worse things get. And you want to know what's even scarier than that? Looking at current trends of church-goers in the U.S., it's only going to get worse.

An entire generation is turning its back on God. Don't let society or fads or making others feel "good" stop you from Biblical truth. Stand up for what's right. Put your hand on the Bible and speak the truth—the truth God spoke from His own lips. It can transform your life, heal your soul, and fill you with unending love.

The Bible is the greatest book ever written, but it's only a matter of time before society throws it into the flames.

Will you be strong and courageous and act on its truths, or will you let God take a backseat while our broken culture drives your life, continually pushing the line to encompass its own "truth?"

Please pray on that, and know I'm praying boldness for each and every one of you. Epic followers of God faced lions, armies, kings, Jericho, and even death, but they didn't back down. And what are we facing in America? *Cancellation?!* Give me a break. They may destroy the Book, but they can't cancel a truth that's been the same yesterday, today, and forever (Hebrews 13:8). God's truth was here before us and it will be here long after us. *Their* truth? It changes every day.

You pick, but I know what side of the line I'm on.

Okay, lights are flickering. Back to our seats.

Intermission is over.

Politics

The Old Testament

- Exodus 20:2–6: "I am the Lord your God, who brought you out of Egypt, out of the land of slavery. You shall have no other gods before Me. You shall not make for yourself an idol in the form of anything in heaven above or on the earth beneath or in the waters below. You shall not bow down to them or worship them; for I, the Lord your God, am a jealous God, punishing the children for the sins of the father to the third and fourth generation of those who hate Me, but showing love to a thousand generations of those who will love Me and keep My commandments."

- Psalm 9:7–8: "The Lord reigns forever; He has established His throne for judgment. He will judge the world in righteousness; He will govern the people with justice."

- Proverbs 29:26: "Many seek an audience with a ruler, but it is from the Lord that man gets justice."

- Isaiah 8:12–13: "Do not call conspiracy everything that these people call a conspiracy; do not fear what they fear, and do not dread it. The Lord Almighty is the one you are to regard as holy, He is the one you are to fear, He is the one you are to dread."

The Most Offensive Book Ever Written

The New Testament

- Mark 12:14-17: "They came to Him and said, 'Teacher, we know that you are a man of integrity. You aren't swayed by others, because you pay no attention to who they are; but you teach the way of God in accordance with the truth. Is it right to pay taxes to Caesar or not? Should we pay or shouldn't we?' But Jesus knew their hypocrisy. 'Why are you trying to trap me?' He asked. 'Bring me a denarius and let me look at it.' They brought the coin, and He asked them, 'Whose portrait is this? And whose inscription?' 'Caesar's,' they replied. Then Jesus said to them, 'Give to Caesar what is Caesar's and to God what is God's.' And they were amazed at Him."

- Acts 5:27-29: "Having brought the apostles, they made them appear before the Sanhedrin to be questioned by the high priest. 'We gave you strict orders not to teach in this name,' he said. 'Yet you have filled Jerusalem with your teaching and are determined to make us guilty of this man's blood.' Peter and the other apostles replied: 'We must obey God rather than men!'"

- Romans 13:1: "Everyone must submit himself to the governing authorities, for there is no authority except that which God has established. The authorities that exist have been established by God."

- Romans 13:7: "Give everyone what you owe him: If you owe taxes, pay taxes; if revenue, then revenue; if respect, then respect; if honor, then honor."

- Titus 3:1-2: "Remind the people to be subject to rulers and authorities, to be obedient, to be ready to do whatever is good, to slander no one, to be peaceable and considerate, and to show true humility toward all men."

God is not a politician and Jesus was not a Democrat or a Republican.

Politics

Looking at these verses, the Bible tells us to respect our governments. We're told to pay our taxes, be obedient to authority, and give everyone what they're owed.

For most of us, that sounds simple enough: we'll pay our taxes, respect laws, and keep up our end of a bargain. Here comes the tough one, though: we're also told to submit to our leaders because God established them where they are . . . I don't know about you, but that's easier said than done.

For some us, we rejected Donald Trump as our President; for others, we reject Joe Biden as our President. I love how it's explained to us in the Bible, though, that God put our leaders where they are—*on purpose* (see previously referenced verse Romans 13:1). That's something easy to read, but hard to comprehend.

Our leaders have been placed where they are *deliberately*. God has plans for them. It's easy to only focus on presidents, but our congressmen, house representatives, governors, mayors, and aldermen have all been purposefully placed where they are. It's not by accident or fluke. Everyone with some sort of political power is exactly where they're supposed to be. It's part of God's plan.

But check this out: just because God places someone, doesn't mean He's placed that person to thrive. We've all had poor co-workers, bad bosses, and selfish leaders. It's the same with politics. Although God places someone (and has established that person), it doesn't mean that person is necessarily there for good; all we have to do is look at Israel's kings in the Old Testament. After David, each generation of kings got worse and worse.

Why, though? Why did God allow that, and why does He continue to place people with poor morals and/or leadership skills in strong political positions? The simple and extremely complex answer is this: it's His will.

God has a plan far beyond ours. With His people—the Israelites—they had poor leaders that led them to getting overtaken by the Assyrians and Babylonians and placed in exile (2 Kings 17:23 and Jeremiah 29:1). From an outside perspective, how horrible, right? How horrible that God's very own people could go down such an immoral path and have such terrible, corrupt leadership that would lead to them getting overtaken by pagan countries with pagan governments!

But the story didn't stop there.

God's will is far beyond ours and He had a plan. While the Israelites were in captivity, He was already planning the coming of His Son. Israel needed to be overtaken to fulfill prophecy (Jeremiah 25:11–14) and set the stage for the coming Christ.

Why is all that significant now? When we look at our politicians and leaders, we might be disgusted, but know this: God's not done. He has a plan that we can't see, and He is able to make water flow from rocks (Exodus 17:5–7). In Isaiah 61:3a, it says, "And provide for those who grieve in Zion—to bestow on them a crown of beauty instead of ashes, the oil of gladness instead of mourning, and a garment of praise instead of a spirit of despair." God is able to make beauty from ashes, no matter the person calling the shots.

God's will is not our will and we may *never* understand why He does what He does; however, I also know no matter how terrible things look to us, when it comes to our politicians and leaders, God *indeed* has a plan and He is able to take even the worst scenario and turn it into an amazing triumph in His name.

We may never understand it ("Why is Trump President? Why is Pelosi Speaker of the House?"), but God tells us, "Have I not commanded you? Be strong and courageous. Do not be terrified; do not be discouraged, for the Lord your God will be with you wherever you go" (Joshua 1:9). We are not to be scared or afraid; instead, we're supposed to be brave and put our trust in Him and His plan. He's got this. He knows what's coming next. We don't. Let's trust the Man with the map.

But even if we grasp that, here's something else: We need to stop identifying ourselves—first—by our political parties; more than anything, if you're a Christian, that's where your identity should come from.

Strap in, boys and girls, this one is going to get bumpy:

God predates our politics and policies. His first written law came in the form of the Ten Commandments (Exodus 20) handed down to Moses; these were given to get all of the Israelites on the same page. The Ten Commandments were God's law to erase any habits or ideologies His chosen people had picked up while slaves in Egypt.

Further on there were dozens of other laws and guidelines given in the Pentateuch, then even further along Jesus modified some of the laws originally given to the Israelites.

All of that happened pre-Democrat and pre-Republican; God's law came before our political parties and affiliations.

I'm hitting on this point because we try to jam God into our political boxes, don't we? We say things like, "If Jesus was alive, He'd vote Republican" or "Jesus would be pro-Socialist" or "Jesus was a feminist." None of that is even relevant: instead of trying to place God in one of our boxes, why don't we try to fit into His?

I'm going to tell you right now, God doesn't check one of our political boxes. Look at your political party; does it follow God's law *100% of the time*? Where does it stand on gay marriage? Abortion? Capital punishment? Loving your neighbor? We try to cram Jesus into our political agendas; we try to weaponize Him and the Gospel, but all that does is drive people away.

We're so married to our political parties. We identify as "Democrat" or "Republican" or "Green Party," but I want to start identifying as a born-again believer in Jesus Christ. That's what needs to come first.

We're all told the lie that politics will save us and if our person is in the White House, then all our problems will go away for four years. Our political leaders are just people, though. They're sinners. Once we start putting our hope and trust in them, we're setting ourselves up for failure, and it doesn't matter what party you're a part of! But when you put your trust in God and His plan, you find peace, reassurance, and stability,

Politics has become a warzone. A lot of us are careful about even hanging out with people from the opposite party. We go into those relationships with prejudices, and that's what society wants: one party is racist, the other isn't. One party wants to give America away, the other doesn't. Politics nowadays (ironically) burns more bridges than it creates. In America, it's Democrat vs. Republican, and we've all seen it: It gets really nasty.

As a society, when we put so much faith in politics, churches become known by their political affiliations, and what a victory for the Devil that is. "I'm not going to that church; it's too Democrat. I'm not going to that church; it's too Conservative." Churches shouldn't be politically motivated, *but* they shouldn't hesitate to address sin in the world.

When countries start bombing each other, the Church should say something. When there is blatant racism, the Church should condemn it. When there's violence and rioting, the Church should stand against it. All of these seem obvious until you drag in the political motivation. "Well, what is that church thinking politically to say that?" No, we want people to say, "What is that church thinking Biblically to say that?"

Churches and Christians, politics need to come after Biblical truth. Politics are important—I'm not saying they're not—but you know what's sobering? What if someone who needs Jesus, needs the Bible, and needs to hear hope, won't go into a church because they're preaching or commenting on politics? Is that our job? I know that's a politicians' job, that's why they're politicians, but in the church, our job is to cross lines and reach people.

God doesn't identify us by our political party. We won't get to Heaven and hear Jesus say, "Republicans over there, Democrats over there, and Green Party, you're way down there." Instead, we'll be identified by if we know Jesus or not. We need to stop seeing and judging people by their flags, shirts, and bumper stickers, and start identifying them by who needs Jesus; it doesn't matter if they voted Trump, Biden, or anyone else.

Writing this, you want to know something, it doesn't matter if I'm a Republican or Democrat. You might want to know, but it honestly doesn't matter. My identity doesn't come from who I cast my single vote for in November every couple years. My identity is rooted in the truth of Jesus Christ; that's what's most important to me, and that's where all my other decisions stem—political, social, economic, and so on.

Politics

Society wants to rip us apart. Our news stations love when we're in conflict; it's great coverage. They'll preach praise for their candidate and smear the opposing party's. But what does the Bible say? Put God first and follow *His* Law (Deuteronomy 10:17-20). His Law is more important than anything that comes out of Capitol Hill.

Just because a human law says abortion, gay marriage, and execution is legal, it doesn't mean it's right in God's eyes.

Don't let politics and fear guide you. Both parties are going to make it seem—*always*—like it's the end of the world . . . but it's really not. Jesus fell asleep on a boat that went through a wicked storm, a storm so bad the disciples thought they were going to drown (Mark 4:35-41); if He wasn't worried about it, I don't want to be worried about it, either. His plan is unfolding all around us. Let's focus our eyes on Him, and put our hope and trust in Him, and not in our politicians—*especially not in our politicians.*

"But should Christians vote?" Absolutely! Your voice counts—even though only for a single vote. However, here comes my challenge to you: look up your party and their beliefs and then cross reference those beliefs with what the Bible says (God's Law comes first). If your party has more similarities with the Bible than another party, there's your answer. If your party differs more with the Bible than another party, then maybe it's time to reassess your party.

Like I said earlier, there is no "Christian" party; there is no party based 100% on God's Word. It's up to you to make the best decision you can based on the knowledge you have.

Learn what the Bible says, pray for discernment and guidance, then vote from there.

> If any of you lacks wisdom, you should ask God, who gives generously to all without finding fault, and it will be given to you. (James 1:5)

Forgiveness

The Old Testament

- Leviticus 19:18: "Do not seek revenge or bear a grudge against one of your people, but love your neighbor as yourself. I am the Lord."
- Psalm 103:12: "As far as the east is from the west, so far has He removed our transgressions from us."
- Proverbs 17:9: "He who covers over an offense promotes love, but whoever repeats the matter separates close friends."
- Isaiah 1:18b: "Though your sins are like scarlet, they shall be as white as snow; though they are red as crimson, they shall be like wool."
- Isaiah 43:25: "I, even I, am He who blots out your transgressions, for My own sake, and remembers your sins no more."

The New Testament

- Matthew 5:7: "Blessed are the merciful, for they will be shown mercy."
- Luke 17:3b: "If your brother sins, rebuke him, and if he repents, forgive him."

- John 13:34–35: "A new command I give you: Love one another. As I have loved you, so you must love one another. By this all men will know that you are My disciples, if you love one another."
- Ephesians 4:32: "Be kind and compassionate to one another, forgiving each other, just as in Christ God forgave you."
- Colossians 3:13: "Bear with each other and forgive whatever grievances you may have against one another. Forgive as the Lord forgave you."

Be merciful.

If we were a society of mercy, grace, and forgiveness, I wouldn't be writing this section right now. I'd be in bed getting a decent night's sleep. But we're not a society of mercy, grace, and forgiveness, so here I am, and here we are.

In order for something to be canceled in our current culture, it usually has to check one (or both) of the following boxes: 1) It's offensive (often what is offensive in this case isn't a sin or objective), and/or 2) When someone has indeed said or done something wrong, examples being hateful emails, cheating scandals, or taking money under the table.

Where society cancels these individuals and buries them for their sins, shouldn't we, as Christians, instead reach out and show mercy? It's pretty apparent what the Bible and Jesus say: Forgive. Forgive. Forgive.

The mercilessness in our society is driven by politicians, news stations, actors, musicians, late night talk show hosts, and social media (just to name a few). As a society, we love when someone makes a mistake—we just love it. We love pinning that person down and jumping on their back, letting them know we know they screwed up and that we'll never forget their mistake.

Are we honestly a society where someone can't make a *single* mistake? "She posted this—cancel her." "He said that—cancel him." We assume when someone fails, that person is a failure. Is that a true way to gauge someone, though? Should a single mistake categorize someone as "broken," "horrible," or "racist?" Society would say "yes." Jesus would say "no."

Can you imagine how doomed all of us would be if Jesus lived by the world's standard? Each one of us makes mistakes—thousands of mistakes a day—and Jesus sees them all. By the world's standard, that's plenty more than enough to condemn us to a lifetime of shame and misery. When we belong to Christ, though, and are truly His children, He can see past our mistakes and see His blood that was spilt for them (Exodus 12:1-30 illustrates this powerfully).

In John 15:12, Jesus tells His disciples, "Love each other as I have loved you." That's the kind of love we're supposed to bring into the world. And how does Jesus love us? With tenderness, unending grace, and a gentleness this world can't fathom. We're not called to cancel. The majority of the time, more than justice, we need to show forgiveness.

We talked about some of this in the *Capital Punishment* segment, and a lot of us are coming in hot out of the *Politics* section, but isn't there a real human part of us that doesn't want to forgive? We *want* to hold a grudge. We want to remember that person's fault. We want to remember what politician said what, what company promoted what, what person funded what, and that's how we'll judge them. I fall into this trap far too often, especially lately after this past political season. But that's how society judges; God commands us to to be better.

You and I both make mistakes. Can you imagine the ruthlessness and unforgiveness *we* deserve? We have all said and done things. If we're honest, we should all be canceled. It's funny watching these politicians, news stations, hosts, companies, and actors/musicians going at it, acting like they're all perfect and never make mistakes. We're all human and every one of us has done something cancelable. In fact, if we had any chance of being perfect, do you think God would have sent His only Son into the world to die in agony on a cross for us? No!

Instead of hating, what if we left justice to God and forgave the person? Truly, nine out of ten times, whoever has wronged us won't ask for forgiveness, but we can forgive them anyway. Let's not let someone else's sin contaminate our drinking water.

Now, I'm not saying you have to like that person or approve of their actions, but I am saying we're commanded by Jesus to show that person a little love and forgiveness because each one of us is given an abundance of it from Him above.

But why? Why should we forgive? Why can't we jump on society's bandwagon and judge ruthlessly with an iron fist? It's fun, it's often deserved, and it makes us feel a bit better about ourselves. So, why?

Because I—*we*—need forgiveness more than anyone. Romans 3:23 says, "For all have sinned and fall short of the glory of God." *All.* In this case, "all" is a pronoun, taking the place of names—your name. My name. Their name. We have sinned and fallen short. It's not our job to condemn. It's our job to be gentle, love, and forgive.

Let's let God judge. Hebrews 9:27 talks about the judgment to come. Thankfully judgment isn't our job, because we're terrible at it.

Now focus, because this bit is important here: When we forgive, we're not saying that particular action is okay, but we're saying that person still has worth and value from God. We don't have to agree with or befriend them, but let's show some mercy. Hurting people hurt others. Instead of ostracizing them in their lowest moments, what if we instead surrounded them with the love and compassion of Jesus.

We can't change *anybody's* life, but Jesus can. When someone makes a mistake, let's pray for them, encourage them to right their wrong (through counseling, direct forgiveness, etc.), and show them Jesus' mercy, because when we show them Jesus' mercy, we show them Jesus.

When society sees mercy out of us, they see the difference the love of Jesus can make: Paul killed Christians, Jonah couldn't stand the people he was called to help, and Joseph's brothers left him for dead, but there was redemption to be found for each of them. In a merciless culture, mercy is attractive.

The Most Offensive Book Ever Written

If we were called to be perfect, we wouldn't need grace, but we're not expected to live flawless lives; it's a human impossibility. We need mercy for our trillions of sins, and so do those around us; let's give it to them and remember: We need Jesus' mercy just as much.

> If we claim to be without sin, we deceive ourselves and the truth is not in us. (1 John 1:8)

Pre-Marital Sex

The Old Testament

- Genesis 2:24: "For this reason a man will leave his father and mother and be united to his wife, and they will become one flesh."
- Exodus 22:16: "If a man seduces a virgin who is not pledged to be married and sleeps with her, he must pay the brideprice, and she shall be his wife."
- Deuteronomy 22:21: "She shall be brought to the door of her father's house and there the men of her town shall stone her to death. She has done a disgraceful thing in Israel by being promiscuous while still in her father's house. You must purge the evil from among you."
- Jeremiah 3:1: "'If a man divorces his wife and she leaves him and marries another man, should he return to her again? Would not the land be completely defiled? But you have lived as a prostitute with many lovers—would you now return to me?' declares the Lord."

The New Testament

- Mark 10:6–9 "But at the beginning of creation God 'made them male and female.' 'For this reason a man will leave his father and mother and be united to his wife, and the two will become one flesh.' So they are no longer two, but one. Therefore what God has joined together, let man not separate."

- 1 Corinthians 6:16: "Do you not know that he who unites himself with a prostitute is one with her in body? For it is said, 'The two will become one flesh.'"

- 1 Corinthians 7:2–3: "But since there is so much immorality, each man should have his own wife, and each woman her own husband. The husband should fulfill his marital duty to his wife, and likewise the wife to her husband."

- Ephesians 5:3: "But among you there must not be even a hint of sexual immorality, or of any kind of impurity, or of greed, because these are improper for God's holy people."

- 1 Thessalonians 4:3–5: "It is God's will that you should be sanctified; that you should avoid sexual immorality; that each of you should learn to control his own body in a way that is holy and honorable, not in passionate lust like the heathen, who do not know God."

Sex is fun, and doesn't God want us to have fun? Well, when it comes to pre-marital sex, no—no He does not.

With the above being stated, why do we have it all messed up? Why are we having pre-marital sex, post-divorce sex, cyber sex, phone sex, and the rest? Because we've lost sight of what the Bible says and are instead focusing on what society says is "okay."

"Tim, come out of the 19th century, bro. We're having sex now. We're liberated!" One of the things I love best about God's Word: It doesn't change. It's flawless and it was put together perfectly.

God put laws in place to prevent premarital sex because look what it can lead to: pregnancy without a plan, disease for a lifetime, loss of self-worth, risk of shared personal videos/pictures, and traumatic experiences inside and outside the bedroom. But maybe most of all, God designed sex to be a shared connection between husband and wife—a bond, union, and blood covenant.

Pre-Marital Sex

"But sex is fun and it feels good and everyone is doing it." Christians—we're called to be different!

Society loves sex and pumps it everywhere it can, like the heart pushing blood through the body. It's everywhere, and it's more than just sex; there's what alludes to sex: young girls dressed and dancing provocatively, short videos on social media of certain trends, and even clothing advertisements for jeans. Sex sells sex and it's everywhere!

Friends, we need to do better here, and this isn't me pointing the finger like I'm better than any of you; this is me saying I'm right there with you and *I* need to do better, too. I don't need to watch that short video, click on that advertisement, or read that article. It can only lead to a real mess of trouble, and it's disrespectful to my wife.

Single people, it's hard to abstain from sex, but it's possible. I was the thirty-year-old virgin . . . and it sucked! I wanted this, that, and the other thing, but I fought daily: my wife and I bought purity rings, I watched sermons on staying abstinent, and I even kept my "Don't Have Sex Until You're Married" card they handed me freshman year of high school. My point in sharing is this: it's *extremely* difficult to remain pure in this culture, but it's possible, and others are fighting the battle right alongside you.

I'm not going to lie and say I've never seen porn, looked at a dirty magazine, or exchanged revealing images. I have and I'm a sinner. But I picked myself up and fought, even though I slipped in spots.

We live in a hyper-sexualized society, to a point where some high schools are stocking their bathrooms with condoms. With messages like that, and with society more or less encouraging sex at *any* age, it's not hard to see why Christians have flown off the rails. There are mixed messages cutting back and forth everywhere, but fortunately, for us, it stops with God's Word: He's made us aware that sex should be saved until marriage (see previously referenced verses 1 Corinthians 7:2–3, Ephesians 5:3, and 1 Thessalonians 4:3–5).

From experience, this was a particularly hard law from God to keep, especially with adolescent hormones, but I was taught in church that sex was special and should be saved. Church saved me on this one. Had God's Word not been taught to me and encouraged in church, it's more than likely I'd have had sex before marriage.

We need to know Biblical truth and then pass it along. Not only that, we need to encourage our brothers and sisters who are fighting in the trenches every day, trying to hold onto their purity in a society that is trying to rip it away from them. Our youth needs our encouragement and guidance. *We* need to be the examples. If they have no one to look up to, why would they not follow in our own sin-laden tracks? We need to fight our sinful urges, not only for us, but for others—we need to be the difference this world so desperately needs.

Honestly, outside of marriage, is sex worth it? What is gained? I can't think of much. But when you put sex inside of marriage, where it belongs, what a symbol it becomes—two becoming one flesh, a perfect fit for each other, the bride and the bridegroom, pure for each other.

Think of your future husband or wife. Do it for them. Give them a gift of *priceless* value. Let them know they mattered before you ever knew them.

Think of your future kids. They'll come to you with questions, too. How encouraging to look them in the eye and say, "I know it's hard to save yourself for marriage, but if *I* can do it, you definitely can."

Purity until marriage is not a popular view by any means. You might hear the words "prude," "virgin (in a derogatory sense, of course)," or "old-fashioned" thrown your way, but that's okay. You're being ridiculed for God and carrying your cross, and one day you'll receive a reward in Heaven (Matthew 5:12).

Etched on the inside of my purity ring was the phrase *True Love Waits*. What a statement to stand up against the swarming locusts of society. And that's where the conversation ends. If your partner isn't onboard with purity, then they're not for you, just another name you can scratch through while you're seeking your future spouse.

You don't want an unplanned pregnancy. You don't want an STD. You don't want to lose your self-worth, feel pressured, or have someone post a video/picture of you. But I'll tell you what you *do* want: a connection between your spouse that you only get one shot at keeping. One shot. No comparisons. No past experiences. No regret.

Brothers and sisters, be brave, be bold, and be courageous. In spite of society's lies and laws, follow God's plan: He designed sex, loves sex, and designated it to be shared with you and only *one* other person—your spouse.

Hold the line.

> Blessed are you when people insult you, persecute you and say all kinds of evil against you because of Me. (Matthew 5:11)

Human Idols

The Old Testament

- Exodus 20:3: "You shall have no other gods before Me."
- Leviticus 19:4: "Do not turn to idols or make gods of cast metal for yourselves. I am the Lord your God."
- Psalm 16:4a: "The sorrows of those will increase who run after other gods."
- Isaiah 42:8: "I am the Lord; that is My name! I will not give My glory to another or praise to idols."
- Isaiah 43:17-18: "From the rest he makes a god, his idol; he bows down to it and worships. He prays to it and says, 'Save me; you are my god.' They know nothing, they understand nothing; their eyes are plastered over so they cannot see, and their minds closed so they cannot understand."

The New Testament

- Matthew 6:24a: "No one can serve two masters. Either he will hate the one and love the other, or he will be devoted to the one and despise the other."
- 1 Corinthians 10:14: "Therefore, my dear friends, flee from idolatry."

- Galatians 4:8: "Formerly, when you did not know God, you were slaves to those who by nature are not gods."
- Galatians 5:19-20a: "The acts of the sinful nature are obvious: sexual immorality, impurity and debauchery; idolatry and witchcraft."
- 1 John 5:21: "Dear children, keep yourselves from idols."

Most of us don't worship animals, ritual poles, or statues/carvings (like they did 2,000+ years ago), but we still have our idols today, don't we?

We have human idols: politicians, news anchors, athletes, celebrities, and dare I say *church leaders*. For a lot of us, we turn to our idols for advice before we turn to God; we're quicker to follow their lead than we are to examine God's Word, and that needs to change.

Yep—I'm again speaking from experience here. I've listened to political leaders, church leaders, favorite actors and musicians, and after they said something, I'd be like, "Yeah! That's it! That's the truth. I'll believe it and follow it." Every time I did that, though, I blew it; it was like I was asking the employee throwing out the trash for something when I could have instead asked the CEO.

We're seeing more and more of this in the media: actors, musicians, and athletes take a stand and support something, and then so many of us say, "Well, if they say it's 'okay,' then it's 'okay' and I support it." Again, we're not talking to the CEO—we're listening to a base-level employee's opinion.

If an actor, musician, athlete, or even a major organization comes out and supports something—especially if they are people or organizations we hold in high regard—the first thing we need to do is cross-check their support/opinion with the Bible: is what they're saying/supporting Biblically based? Instead of following what God and Jesus have said, we're quick to follow what one of our "idols" supports: "If they're for gay marriage, then I'm for gay marriage. If they're for a sexualized movie about kid dancers, then I'm for that same movie. If they're against the police, then I'm against the police."

And I've been there—many, many times—and I know what it's like to lead with emotion over Biblical fact. We put someone else in God's place and that person's opinion is more important than His.

For most of us, this becomes blatantly apparent with politics. If that politician says we need to close the borders, then we need to close the borders. If that politician says we need to open the borders, then we need to open the borders. So many of us get caught-up basing our beliefs and ideologies on human thoughts and rhetoric, which are ironically often based on popularity and a particular agenda—not God's Word.

We treat our politicians like gods. Trump will save us. Biden will save us. Bernie will save us (eh). But here is the ultimate truth in all of this (I hope you're ready for it): If you put your faith and trust in people, you will be let down by them 10/10 times; if you put your faith and trust in God, you'll *never* be let down. As a society, we have put *way* too much faith, hope, and trust in regular people and not in the Savior of the world.

Not only is this a media and political thing, but also a church thing. How many of us have abandoned what the Bible says (are we even reading our Bibles anymore?) and just listening to what the leaders of our churches say? Church leaders are people, too, and they're going to let you down 10/10 times as well!

I'm from Illinois and we've had major church-leader scandals. Congregations have been torn apart because of scandals. People have left the church permanently as a result. Here's the problem with that: was their allegiance to God or to that one person? Who's been God in *your* life? Who are you listening to? Who is deciding things for you?

We need to respect our leaders, but don't always take their word for it. It's okay to cross-check them with the Bible. Is what they're saying and how they're acting Biblically-based? Is it from God? Is it for God's purpose or their own?

Catholics, this next bit might pinch a little, but hear me out: the Catholic Church, too, has put a lot of faith in their clergy, and so many congregants have been burned by that faith. People will always—*at some point*—let you down! Always. Never put your full faith in people; they don't deserve the pedestal of God in your life. You know who does? God (Hebrews 13:5-6).

In Matthew 23:9-12, it says, "And do not call anyone on earth 'father,' for you have one Father, and He is in heaven. Nor are you to be called 'teacher,' for you have one Teacher, the Christ. The greatest among you will be your servant. For whoever exalts himself will be humbled, and whoever humbles himself will be exalted."

God is father—*the* Father. Man is clothed in dirty rags. Priests and clergy may be great people, but they are just that—people. Seek Him first (Matthew 6:33).

And my Catholic friends, for those of you still in attendance after that, let's dive a little deeper. Look in your Bibles: Mary, the saints, and the angels are not God, either. I see no Biblical proof where they should be prayed to, worshiped, or have ceremonies held in their honor. I see *no* Biblical proof. I see Biblical proof where God says, "You shall have no other gods before me," and that's it. Again, why ask the kid cleaning out the grease trays when you can go right to God instead? I don't believe Mary or St. Paul or the others can hear your prayers. They're in Heaven worshiping God (Revelation 7:9-10). Were they great people? Absolutely. But that's it, and people don't deserve our worship.

For some, that may be jarring, and here's why: in our churches, so many of us do what we're told without asking why. Instead, we need to read our Bibles every day. Read it from cover to cover.

Learn why you believe what you believe. For a lot of you, you'll walk away from reading the Bible going, "Why in the world have I been doing X, Y, and Z all these years?" For so many, beliefs have been based on tradition and not Biblical truth.

Tradition is not our God. Mary is not our God. Biden is not our God. The leaders of BLM are not our God. The Republican Party is not our God. Bill Hybels or James MacDonald are not our God. The Pope (who is also just a human) is not our God. Tebow is not our God (how could you not like Tebow, though?). Family is not our God. Our spouses are not our God. And I am not my own God.

We need to take a serious look at our pedestals and see who we've placed there. Who is guiding our lives? Who is most important? If it's not God, it's time to let Him retake command.

People are not worthy to run our lives; but what if we allowed God to run our lives, the same God who loved us enough to send His only Son, Jesus Christ, to die in our place?

God is the only one to be absolutely listened to, obeyed, and lived in reverence of.

> That at the name of Jesus every knee should bow, in heaven and on earth and under the earth, and every tongue confess that Jesus Christ is Lord, the glory of God the Father. (Philippians 2:10–11)

Other Religions

The Old Testament

- Genesis 1:1: "In the beginning God created the heavens and the earth."
- Exodus 20:3: "You shall have no other gods before me."
- Exodus 22:20: "Whoever sacrifices to any god other than the Lord must be destroyed."
- Joshua 24:14: "Now fear the Lord and serve Him with all faithfulness. Throw away the gods your forefathers worshiped beyond the River and in Egypt, and serve the Lord."
- 1 Kings 18:21: "Elijah went before the people and said, 'How long will you waver between two opinions? If the Lord is God, follow Him; but if Baal is God, follow him.' But the people said nothing."

The New Testament

- John 3:18: "Whoever believes in Him is not condemned, but whoever does not believe stands condemned already because he has not believed in the name of God's one and only Son."
- John 14:6: "Jesus answered, 'I am the way and the truth and the life. No one comes to the Father except through Me.'"

- 1 Corinthians 8:5–6: "For even if there are so called gods, whether in heaven or on earth (as indeed there are many 'gods' and many 'lords'), yet for us there is but one God, the Father, from whom all things came and for whom we live; and there is but one Lord, Jesus Christ, through whom all things came and through whom we live."

- Galatians 1:6–8: "I am astonished that you are so quickly deserting the One who called you by the grace of Christ and are turning to a different gospel—which is really no gospel at all. Evidently some people are throwing you into confusion and are trying to pervert the gospel of Christ. But even if we or an angel from heaven should preach a gospel other than the one we preached to you, let him be eternally condemned!"

- Revelation 1:8: "'I am the Alpha and the Omega,' says the Lord God, 'who is, and who was, and who is to come, the Almighty.'"

Our society says all religions are fine and acceptable, but the Bible says there is only one Truth.

The fact of the matter is there can only be one *true* religion. You've seen the bumper stickers; society is pushing us all to "coexist." While we should be able to coexist and live peacefully amongst each other, there can only be one truth, and that truth is found in the Bible: God created the heavens and the earth and Jesus Christ is the answer to eternity in Heaven. There you have it. Need I go on?

All religions can't be correct—they each have different gods with different laws from different origins. They clash and contradict each other. Only one religion can be true.

"So, are you actually telling me Christianity is the only *true* religion? Are you really that bold to make that statement?"

Yes!

Christianity is the only true religion, Jesus is the only way to Heaven, and when we die we'll be face to face with God (Revelation 20:11–12).

"But how can you say that and actually *believe* it? There's so many religions out there. How is Christianity correct and the rest wrong?" From my own recent studies, I've come to believe this extremely important truth: when it comes to what you choose to believe, you need to know why you believe it.

Dig in and learn. Learn about geographical history. Learn what ancient writings say about the life of Jesus. Learn what history has to say about the Bible. Learn, learn, learn!

From the studies I've done, I've concluded what the Bible says is true. I've concluded God created the earth perfectly, humans brought sin into His perfect world through free will, Jesus Christ was who He said He was (the Son of God), and He indeed died, rose again, ascended, and will return . . . among hundreds of other truths.

I've read many books and listened to countless sermons by various different scholars and researchers, including Lee Strobel, Tony Evans, Patrick Henry Reardon, C.S. Lewis, John Piper, and John Lennox. I did the work to find out why I believe what I believe, and it only *strengthened* my faith.

I believe—without a shadow of a doubt—that what the Bible says is true and accurate. Where other religions have holes, gaps, and lack of evidence, the Bible does not. It is the one Truth. And that's it.

But please don't take my word for it. Do your own research. Find out why *you* believe what you believe. Have no doubts.

"What about Islam, Hinduism, Buddhism, and other religions? What about those who are agnostic or atheist? Are you telling me all of them are wrong and *you* are right?" Absolutely, and I'm betting my eternity on it.

Christians, we can't be wishy-washy here. The world needs us to take a stand. The Christian God is the one we serve. As a Biblical truth, there are no other gods. This isn't about tolerance or acceptance—it's about truth, and there can only be one.

One of my favorite Bible stories is where Elijah challenged the prophets of Baal to a fire-starting contest. Elijah said if pagan god Baal consumes their sacrifice with fire, he's the real god; but if his God lit up the sacrifice in fire, then He's the real God. The challenge was accepted. You can find the entire story in 1 Kings 18:20–39.

Obviously, it didn't go too good for Baal's prophets. They were screaming and cutting themselves—not good times. Needless to say, a fire never came down and burned their sacrifice.

Then it was Elijah's turn. He prayed, "O Lord, God of Abraham, Isaac and Israel, let it be known today that you are God in Israel" (1 Kings 18:36b). Then a fire raged from the sky and consumed Elijah's entire sacrifice and more.

This story has recently found deep meaning for me because of who Elijah prayed to. He didn't pray, "Soft, liberal God who will never punish, come down and do *something*. Oh, and if you can, wear a shirt with a rainbow on it. Yeah, that'd be great. Thanks!" No. He knew exactly who he was praying to—the one and only God. YHWH. The God who spoke to Abraham, blessed Isaac, and prospered Israel. Elijah didn't mince words in His prayer. He called out to *the* God.

Who are we calling out to?

For some Christians, we're trying to bend Jesus, God, and the Bible to fit our social and political agendas. This "new" religion we've created—it's a sham. When you pray, cry out to the true God—the God of Abraham, Isaac, Jacob, and more.

As much as other religions are wrong, so is this "New Christianity"—the Christianity that promotes LGBTQ agendas, offers same sex marriages in their buildings, won't say the word "sin," and says abortion is "okay." This "New Christianity" is *not* of the Bible.

I get it. I get wanting to be accepting, kind, and inclusive. Jesus hung out with sinners. I understand that part of it. But you know what else He did? He called out sin when He saw it. He didn't turn a blind eye to it. He showed love first—absolutely—but then He offered salvation and *a new way of life*.

Let's look at a few times Jesus called out sin: He called out murder (Matthew 5:21-22), adultery (Matthew 5:27-28), divorce (Matthew 5:31-32), robbery (Matthew 21:12-13), hypocrisy (Mark 7:6-8), pride in wealth (Mark 10:23-25), testing God (Luke 4:12), judging others (Luke 6:37), vengeance (Luke 9:53-55), love of money (Luke 16:13), and assassination (John 8:39-41).

OTHER RELIGIONS

Jesus called out sin. He rebuked sin and told His disciples to rebuke it as well: "If a brother or sister sins against you, rebuke them" (Luke 17:3a). We're not supposed to accept or bend an entire belief system so no one feels guilt or shame. We're supposed to speak the truth—Biblical truth—and that's how we help those who don't know right from wrong.

Jesus says in Matthew 18:15, "If a brother or sister sins, go and point out the fault." It's okay to correct and guide! Not every choice everyone makes is okay. Christ was tolerant, but He was also bold and righteous. Our God is described as having a staff to guide and a rod to correct (Psalm 23:4b). Guide and correct, not accept and tolerate.

This false Christianity humans have created must die.

How many of us Christians fall into Christ's words when He said, "You have let go of the commands of God and are holding on to human traditions" (Mark 7:8)? For many of us, we've lost sight of the truth. We've been consumed by the very human ideas of "acceptance" and "tolerance." We've forgotten we can both love and disapprove at the same time, like parents over their children.

When it comes to other religions, the Bible is the one never-changing truth in a society that is constantly changing and pushing the line further and further. God's truths haven't changed—ever—and they won't. Isn't that a relief? God's Word is a rock—*the* rock; everything else is sinking sand (Matthew 7:24–27)—every other religion, belief system, and ideology. Born-again Christianity is the one, never failing truth in this world of chaos and disorder.

But what some Christians are doing now is bending and straining that truth to make it fit the common-day agenda. Don't believe me? How come some churches are only now accepting homosexuality, gay-marriage, and abortion? The Bible as we know it today, adapted from the King James Bible, has been around since 1611, not to mention ancient manuscripts from thousands of years ago. The truth has always been there, but because these topics are gaining more and more momentum within society, and Christian values are becoming more and more unpopular, many Christians feel they have to "catch-up with the times" and "change"

God's Word so it's more "accepting" and "tolerant." Christians, *stop doing this*! Through Biblical truth, we're allowed to stay right where we are, show love, and stand on the firm foundation of the ultimate Truth.

And maybe more than anything, stand behind the Bible. If people attack you for speaking God's truth, they're attacking God—not you. Let Him fight your battles. He's our rock and our fortress. Whom shall we fear (Psalm 18:2–3)?

And as I stated earlier, don't take my word for it. Do your own studies and research. *Know why you believe what you believe.* Compare Christianity to other religions, belief systems, and ideologies. Do your homework. The research, facts, and truth are there. Discover them for yourself.

> Anyone who runs ahead and does not continue in the teaching of Christ does not have God; whoever continues in the teaching has both the Father and the Son. (2 John 1:9)

Heaven

The Old Testament

- 1 Kings 8:30: "Hear the supplication of Your servant and of Your people Israel when they pray toward this place. Hear from Heaven, Your dwelling place, and when You hear, forgive."

- 2 Kings 2:11: "As they were walking along and talking together, suddenly a chariot of fire and horses of fire appeared and separated the two of them, and Elijah went up to Heaven in a whirlwind."

- Psalm 20:6: "Now I know that the Lord saves His anointed; He answers Him from His holy Heaven with the saving power of His right hand."

- Isaiah 65:17: "Behold, I will create new heavens and a new earth. The former things will not be remembered, nor will they come to mind."

- Lamentations 3:41: "Let us lift up our hearts and our hands to God in Heaven."

The Most Offensive Book Ever Written

The New Testament

- Luke 23:42–43: "Then he said, 'Jesus, remember me when You come into Your kingdom.' Jesus answered him, 'I tell you the truth, today you will be with Me in paradise.'"
- John 14:2: "In My Father's house are many rooms; if it were not so, I would have told you. I am going there to prepare a place for you."
- 2 Corinthians 5:1: "Now we know that if the earthly tent we live in is destroyed, we have a building from God, an eternal house in Heaven, not built by human hands."
- Revelation 21:1–3: "Then I saw a new heaven and a new earth, for the first heaven and the first earth had passed away, and there was no longer any sea. I saw the Holy City, the new Jerusalem, coming down out of Heaven from God, prepared as a bride beautifully dressed for her husband. And I heard a loud voice from the throne saying, 'Now the dwelling of God is with men, and He will live with them. They will be His people, and God Himself will be with them and be their God.'"

See also 2 Corinthians 5:1–10 and Revelation chapters 21 and 22 in their entirety.

God is in Heaven and He desires for us to live with Him there; *all* are invited, but not all will answer His call.

Some say everyone goes to Heaven, no matter how you live, what you do, or who your god is. But the Bible says there is only one way: "Jesus answered, 'I am the Way and the Truth and the Life. No one comes to the Father except through Me'" (John 14:6).

We live in a society where few stand up and take responsibility for their actions; it's always somebody else's fault. "I grew up in a broken home, that's why I started using drugs." "I live in the wrong neighborhood/am the wrong race, that's why I can't succeed." "I feel neglected by my spouse, that's why I had an affair." Although complex issues, there is personal responsibility to be taken.

For myself, going through recovery after growing up in an alcoholic home, it would have been easy for me to blame my anxiety, depression, stress, and family members for the hurt I had caused. However, in recovery, you learn to take responsibility and make amends.

All of that is to say, not all of us will be in Heaven. We will be judged by our actions here on earth. There will be consequences for what we did or didn't do—plain and simple. We can't point the finger at anyone else. The decision is *ours* and ours alone.

When God created the world, He created it with free will—a beautiful thing. Because of free will, I can choose what I want to do, where I want to go, and what I'm going to follow. Also because of free will, I can choose to do wrong. Free will = consequence, whether good or bad.

But why did God give us free will? Because He wants us to choose to love and follow Him. Without free will, there is no such thing as love—we'd be programmed drones. God gave us free will so we can freely love, a pure love which is not based on reciprocity, but passionate desire.

With free will, we also have the freedom not to love. We have the freedom to worship whatever gods we want and make harmful and hurtful decisions; *we* make the decision to choose Heaven or not.

Friends, not everyone you know will be in Heaven, because too many of us are not serious about our eternity; so many believe the lie that once we die, we will automatically spend our lives in Heaven because we "deserve it" and did enough good, but that is not the case. Heaven is a choice, and there are eternal spiritual consequences for our decisions made on earth.

"You're saying God would actually *punish* His creation?"

Yes, but it's not God punishing for no reason. In John 3:17, we're told God sent His Son into the world *to save the world*; ultimately it's *our* decision to be punished. We can choose redemption and salvation or we can choose punishment and shame.

"Okay, let's say we understand Heaven is real, it's our choice to get there, and not everyone will choose Heaven; how does one get to Heaven?"

The only way into Heaven is Jesus. Heaven isn't something we earn. Christians, so many of us are confused with this, believing if we do enough good we can earn our way into Heaven. There's no Biblical proof of that. None. How much good is good enough? Do certain bads outweigh certain goods? What if I become a Christian later in life—can I do enough good to make up for decades of bad? No one knows the answers to those questions! Instead, the Bible says, "For it is by grace you have been saved, through faith—and this is not from yourselves, it is the gift of God—not by works, so that no one can boast" (Ephesians 2:8–9).

Look also at the story of the thief on the cross. We don't know much about the man except that he was a thief being crucified for his actions, but also that He trusted in Jesus in his final hour. In response to the man, Jesus said, "Today you will be with me in paradise" (Luke 23:43b). The man didn't have to do anything else. He didn't have to be baptized, do good works, be blessed by a priest, or take communion. All he had to do was believe in Jesus, and because he did, he's worshiping Jesus in Heaven right now.

The story of the thief on the cross simply illustrates that Heaven and eternal life is a *gift* from Jesus. Jesus did the work. The price has been paid. All we have to do is accept it—and when we accept it, that's good enough.

We don't reach Heaven through works, baptism, or communion (again, none of that is Biblically sound); we reach Heaven—*only*—through believing in Jesus Christ as our Lord and Savior. His blood on the cross was the payment. He took our spot. By believing in Him, the Bible tells us we can have eternal life.

> Critical Side Note: Being a Christian is about engaging with Jesus, living for Him, and being forever changed because of Him. It should completely uproot your life and change who you are (Galatians 2:17–20). If you claim to be a Christian and nothing is changed about you, then you should deeply consider if you are truly a Christian.

Heaven

You don't get to live your own way and still be a Christian; it's about surrendering your old self and choosing Him anew each and every day. It's about incredible change and faithful growth. Saying a single prayer and then abandoning God to do your own thing is not salvation.

Brothers and sisters, Heaven is a beautiful place, and if you're a true Christian, you'll spend eternity there worshiping our Lord and Savior. Revelation 21:4 says, "He will wipe every tear from their eyes. There will be no more death or mourning or crying or pain, for the old order of things has passed away."

But only those who believe in Christ for the redemption of their sins will be there. We're terrible, horrible people and we need salvation by Jesus. We're not good enough; nothing we do will ever make us good enough, except allowing Jesus to take our sins and wipe them clean.

If you're a Christian, the Holy Spirit has come down upon you and lives inside you (Acts 2:1-4). The Holy Spirit—part of the Trinity, *part of God*—resides in you, and my Spirit can't wait to get back to Heaven and worship God; it longs to go back home.

"Is that all Heaven is going to be—worship? That sounds lame."

We've all been around people who've embarrassed us. For me, there were times when my dad was drunk and I was out in public with him and I felt completely ashamed, where I wanted to hide my face and just disappear. I wanted to say I didn't even know who he was.

We've all had moments like that to some degree, but where *we* were the ones who deserved to be embarrassed and deserved to be ashamed, where we completely turned our backs on God and did our own thing.

In my life, at my lowest, I had no hope, was sickly, was bawling on the floor of my bedroom, and wasn't able to see a day ahead. Where others might have been embarrassed or ashamed to be with me or know me, that's where God met me. He wasn't ashamed of me. His love is enough to where He met me on that floor, when I had absolutely nothing, and told me I was worth more than I could ever even imagine.

That's why I can't wait to kneel before my King in Heaven and sing His praises forevermore.

Heaven is for *anyone* who accepts Jesus. You can be a murderer on death row and still repent and find Jesus. In fact, Jesus says, "Very truly I tell you, *whoever* hears My word and believes Him who sent Me has eternal life and will not be judged but has crossed over from death to life" (John 5:24).

So don't listen to this world any longer. Your actions have consequences. Find Jesus *now*—His unending love, amazing grace, and faithful salvation—all before it's too late. The stakes couldn't be higher.

> Seek the Lord while He may be found; call on Him while He is near. (Isaiah 55:6)

Hell

The Old Testament

- Psalm 86:13: "For great is Your love toward me; You have delivered me from the depths of the grave."
- Psalm 110:5: "The Lord is at Your right hand; He will crush kings on the day of His wrath."
- Isaiah 66:24: "And they will go out and look upon the dead bodies of those who rebelled against me; their worm will not die, nor will their fire be quenched, and they will be loathsome to all mankind."
- Daniel 12:2: "Multitudes who sleep in the dust of the earth will awake: some to everlasting life, others to shame and everlasting contempt."

The New Testament

- Matthew 25:46: "Then they will go away to eternal punishment, but the righteous to eternal life."
- Mark 9:47–48: "And if your eye causes you to sin, pluck it out. It is better for you to enter the Kingdom of God with one eye than to have two eyes and be thrown into Hell, where 'their worm does not die, and the fire is not quenched.'"

- 2 Thessalonians 1:8–9: "He will punish those who do not know God and do not obey the gospel of our Lord Jesus. They will be punished with everlasting destruction and shut out from the presence of the Lord and from the majesty of His power."
- Revelation 20:15: "If anyone's name was not found written in the Book of Life, he was thrown into the lake of fire."
- Revelation 21:8: "But the cowardly, the unbelieving, the vile, the murderers, the sexually immoral, those who practice magic arts, the idolaters and all liars—their place will be in the fiery lake of burning sulfur. This is the second death."

See also Luke 16:19–31

Hell is real.

Not only is Hell real, but by default, we all have a booked ticket there.

That statement should rattle you.

Mirroring the section on Heaven, there are consequences for our actions, and what we do on earth, in the here and now, will determine whether we spend eternity in Heaven with Jesus or in the horrid depths of Hell.

No one likes to think about Hell. We all try to put it out of our minds. Honestly, look around you: on TV, in your social feeds, in the news; aren't we all living like we have nothing to fear?

But judgment is coming. And it will be righteous. Those who only received a slap on the wrist for their crimes on earth will stand before God. What was done in the dark will be brought to the light (Luke 12:2–3). No wise-cracking, bartering, or deals will be made.

"So, how do you escape Hell?" Your eternity will come down to one thing: What did you do with Jesus?

Look at our society. *Jesus who?* Can you imagine what people would do (atheists, so-called "Christians," and everyone in-between) if they were *convinced* they were going to Hell? I think the chairs would get pretty full on Sundays. But denial, misguidance, and lack of interest still rule. Unfortunately, some of our churches are to blame: Why aren't all churches talking about Hell?

Hell

Especially at larger churches, Hell doesn't pay the bills. As people, it can be really hard to hear we're not living to a certain standard and that there will be consequences for our actions. If I was gambling man, I'd bet the larger the church, the less "Hell talk" there is. We want to hear how great we are, get a little piece of encouragement, and then hit the road. A lot of churches are teaching fluff, but what we need is some gritty red meat.

I don't think Hell should be taught all the time (fire and brimstone and all that), but living in denial of Hell is giving the Devil exactly what he wants. Hell needs to be addressed and it needs to start now. Hell is the elephant in the room. Growing up in a dysfunctional household, we never talked about alcohol or the problem and strain it was; we lived in denial of it. But that's not love and that's not healthy. In churches, sometimes what people need most is hard-love; they don't need a pat on the back or told how great they are—they need a kick in the pants!

As Christians, it's our job to educate. Yes, we need to preach that Jesus saves and rescues, but saves and rescues *from what*? Are we really loving our neighbors if we fail to mention consequences and the cost of living a sinful life?

If all I believed as a Christian is that God is good and Jesus forgives all, would I change my lifestyle much? If it was all sweets and sugar and *Kumbaya*, I'd be living like everyone else. With no consequences, wouldn't we all be living differently? But there *are* consequences. And we will be judged. And for some of us, Hell will be all too real.

Leaders and pastors, it's our duty to educate. Being such, we're called to preach the Bible as it is, not as we would have it, and we'll be judged according to whether we did or not: "Not many of you should presume to be teachers, my brothers, because you know that we who teach will be judged more strictly" (James 3:1). We don't get to pick and choose what to teach. We don't get to talk about the fun things (like peace, joy, and love), but at the same time ignore the hard topics (like Hell, homosexuality, and abortion). If we're called to teach and lead, then we need to dive in and preach the *entire* Bible; not just the bits we like best.

Those in church leadership, plain and simple, we can't be everyone's friend. We can't avoid the hard topics so we don't get negative feedback on our social accounts. At a lot of churches, leaders get on stage, put on a clever song and dance, there's applause, and then everyone goes home. But listen to this: we're not called to be friends; we're called to be leaders. James says, "Anyone who chooses to be a friend of the world becomes an enemy of God" (James 4:4b). Should we make an effort to be warm and cordial with our congregants and guests? Absolutely! But more than that, our chief priority is to speak God's truth, and that's how we love.

However unfortunate, the truth is that Hell is real; not only real, but harrowing.

I heard Bill Wiese speak about Hell (he believed he was sent there in some out-of-body experience), and I don't know whether it actually happened or not, but his descriptions of that horrific place will make your blood run cold, and I'm sure his descriptions pale in comparison to its actuality. People need to know Hell is real and that's where they're headed if they don't choose Jesus. It's never going to be a popular message or one people want to hear, but it's a message they *need* to hear.

Some truths are hard, but I want to be courageous enough to share even the hardest of truths with my non-believing friends. I get it, I really do: It can be hard to talk about Hell and tell someone that's where they're headed, but if you truly love that person, you love them enough to tell them the truth and not just coddle them with watered-down Christianity. I've failed so many times in this area, but I want to continually strive to do better and share the entire truth of the Bible, because someone's eternity is more important than an awkward conversation.

"But why is there Hell?" Like Heaven, because there's free will. Because we have free will, we can choose Jesus or not. It is not God's desire for *any* of us to go to Hell, but He can't intervene and stop us from heading to Hell, because then it's not free will anymore. Our chance to avoid Hell is now. *Right now*. Don't waste this time, chance, and opportunity. You never know when it can be snatched away.

Hell

And churches, this is my plea to you: please start talking about Hell like it's a real place. The Bible—especially the New Testament—does not hold back in describing Hell. Hell is a place of "weeping and gnashing of teeth" (Matthew 13:42), "everlasting destruction" (2 Thessalonians 1:9), and home of the "second death" (Revelation 21:8). This isn't a game. This isn't child's play. You're not doing anyone in your congregation any favors if you're not telling them the entire truth of the Bible. Hell is not canceled. Hell. Is. Real.

I've been around mega churches now for the past 15+ years and I can probably count the total number of Hell sermons I've heard on three fingers. I've heard plenty of messages on miracles, resurrection, eternal hope, and all that other good stuff, but so few on Hell. Too few. Again, preaching the fun stuff is only one side of the balance; without fully understanding what we're being rescued from, the weight of Jesus' ultimate sacrifice doesn't hit its deepest depth. When we accept Jesus, we're rescued from eternal separation, torment, and damnation.

Yeah. This is heavy stuff. And it's not fun talking about it. It's not what people want to hear, but we can't pretend Hell isn't real; we can't live in denial any longer. Church isn't about making people happy so they'll pay the bills and keep the lights on; it's about truth—*the* Truth—and if we're not preaching it, shame on us; we're doing more harm than good.

Before wrapping-up this section, take a moment and feel the weight of what we're actually talking about here.

Take a breath.

"Tim, I took a breath, but still—how can you actually say 'Hell is real?'" Because it is. I wish it wasn't, but this isn't fairytale stuff or ghost stories. This is real life. And in this life there are consequences. The ultimate consequence for living a sinful life, without Jesus there to cover your sins, is eternal separation from God (Matthew 25:41). The Bible is God's Word; every word is inspired by Him.

And friends, I know it's easy to talk sarcastically about Hell, but don't take this lightly. Don't listen to the world; every action *is* being taken note of (Matthew 12:36). There is good and there is evil. Follow Biblical truth and you'll find abundant joy, overwhelming peace, and eternal salvation. Follow anything else and, well, you won't have an excuse when you get there.

> So he called to him, "Father Abraham, have pity on me and send Lazarus to dip the tip of his finger in water and cool my tongue, because I am in agony in this fire." (Luke 16:24)

Jesus

The Old Testament

- Genesis 3:15: "And I will put enmity between you and the woman, and between your offspring and hers; He will crush your head, and you will strike His heel."

- 2 Samuel 7:12-13: "When your days are over and you rest with your fathers, I will raise up your offspring to succeed you, who will come from your own body, and I will establish His kingdom. He is the one who will build a house for My Name, and I will establish the throne of His kingdom forever."

- Isaiah 7:14: "Therefore the Lord Himself will give you a sign: The virgin will be with child and will give birth to a son, and will call Him Immanuel."

- Isaiah 9:6: "For to us a child is born, to us a son is given, and the government will be on His shoulders. And He will be called Wonderful Counselor, Mighty God, Everlasting Father, Prince of Peace."

- Zechariah 9:9: "Rejoice greatly, O Daughter of Zion! Shout, Daughter of Jerusalem! See, your King comes to you, righteous and having salvation, gentle and riding on a donkey, on a colt, the foal of a donkey."

The Most Offensive Book Ever Written
The New Testament

- John 3:16-18: "For God so loved the world that He gave His one and only Son, that whoever believes in Him shall not perish but have eternal life. For God did not send His Son into the world to condemn the world, but to save the world through Him. Whoever believes in Him is not condemned, but whoever does not believe stands condemned already because he has not believed in the name of God's one and only Son."

- Acts 4:11-12: "He is 'the stone you builders rejected which has become the capstone.' Salvation is found in no one else, for there is no other name under Heaven given to men by which we must be saved."

- Philippians 2:8-11: "And being found in appearance as a man, He humbled Himself and became obedient to death—even death on a cross! Therefore God exalted Him to the highest place and gave Him the name that is above every name, that at the name of Jesus every knee should bow, in Heaven and on earth and under the earth, and every tongue confess that Jesus Christ is Lord, to the glory of God the Father."

- 1 Timothy 2:3-6: "This is good, and pleases God our Savior, who wants all men to be saved and to come to a knowledge of the truth. For there is one God and one mediator between God and men, the man Christ Jesus, who gave Himself as a ransom for all men—the testimony given in its proper time."

See also the gospels in their entirety: Matthew, Mark, Luke, and John

Jesus was not just "a good man;" He was the Son of God, and salvation comes only through Him.

With this whole "coexist" movement, we're told Jesus was a good man and great prophet, but that's all He was—a man. The fact of the matter is this, though: Jesus fulfilled over 100 Messianic prophecies, some given 1,500 years before His birth; He was not a Messianic imposter. He was not a magician, sorcerer, or demon. He *was* the Son of God, birthed by a virgin in Bethlehem; He

JESUS

would then grow up to be baptized by His cousin John, have a world-changing ministry for 2-3 years, be betrayed by Judas, die on a cross, and ultimately rise out of His tomb, conquering death forever, and ascend into Heaven—that's who Jesus was.

If you subtract any of that, you're not looking at the Biblical, historically verified Jesus. He was not a myth or legend. He's God's Son who was sent as the ultimate sacrifice, showing love at an unimaginable scale. Watering down any of who Jesus is and what He accomplished on this earth is a travesty.

Don't believe any of what I just claimed? Open the Bible and read the gospels. In addition, read 'The Case for the Real Jesus' by Lee Strobel and 'The Jesus We Missed' by Patrick Henry Reardon—two great reads on the historical account of Jesus, as well as the majesty of who Jesus was and what He accomplished as both God and man simultaneously.

My Jewish, Catholic, and JW friends—Jesus *is* the Son of God. He is the *only* way into Heaven. He is the Messiah who was prophesied to the Jewish people. He is the Way and Truth—no amount of works you do can ever come close to matching up to what He did on the cross, and when He returns, He will call up His people and they will meet Him in the sky, just like how He ascended before Pentecost (Acts 1:11).

"You're telling me God walked on this planet? This is what you *actually* believe? And not only that, but that He would go on to die for the sins of the world?"

I know it sounds incomprehensible, but that's because it is! Jesus' story is honestly the greatest story ever told. He is hope to a broken world and love to a lonely people—He is Christ the Lord (Luke 2:11)! You can have it all—a multi-billion dollar company, great spouse, incredible kids, foundations for the poor, amazing friends, and a phenomenal legacy, but without Jesus, you have *nothing*. This world is not about what we can do; it's about what Jesus already did. He's the only one that can clean your slate of its backlogged sins.

Check to make sure your harnesses are locked, because we're about to get real: Jesus is as offensive today as He was 2,000 years ago. What Jesus taught was radical: inclusion and equality across ethnic and gender lines, salvation through Himself alone, and that He was indeed the Son of God. What people are so offended by today is... well... everything He stood for!

We'll take this piece by piece: a lot of "Christians" today like Jesus, but they're not big God fans. And why? They like the mercy and forgiveness of Jesus, but don't like the righteous justice of God. The problem with that is that Jesus is part of the Trinity: God the Father, God the Son, and God the Holy Spirit. If you follow one part and not the others, are you really a Christian?

So many of us want to have our cake and eat it, too. We say we follow Jesus but don't fully accept what He stands for. If we are truly Christ followers, then we're against abortion, sexual immorality, unforgiveness, and everything else we've talked about. Jesus was against these things; most of the previous sections have direct quotes from Him!

It's easy to see why Jesus was murdered: He was killed because He disrupted the Pharisees' world (the religious leaders of the time). And there are so many today wanting to cancel Jesus for the same reason—because what He stands for doesn't go with the flow. He's disruptive.

Friends, we can no longer be ashamed of the Bible and gospel. We're the last line of defense. Once all of us Bible-based Christians fold, the Devil wins and "New Christianity" will reign supreme—a Christianity based on thoughts and feelings with zero Spiritual impact.

But now, here's the ultimate question: Are you following the Biblical Jesus, who condemned, rebuked, and called out, or are you following the fluff version of Jesus that packs the seats on Sunday?

Are *you* ready to pay the cost and follow the Biblical Jesus?

Even in Jesus' time there was a cost to following Him; this is nothing new. In John chapter six, Jesus was preaching at a synagogue in Capernaum. He had some young "believers" there, people who had seen Him do miracles and incredible feats, but that was all they wanted more of. Jesus, however, said, "I am the bread of life. He who comes to Me will never go hungry, and he

JESUS

who believes in Me will never be thirsty. But as I told you, you have seen Me and still you do not believe" (John 6:35–36). They wanted Jesus "the miracle worker and healer;" they didn't want to have to fully surrender everything and follow Him. They wanted a neutered version of Jesus, but Jesus was essentially telling them it's not about the miracles or works, but about the life He brought, and they didn't want it: "From this time many of His disciples turned back and no longer followed Him" (John 6:66). They didn't want to do the work or follow His teachings; they wanted to be entertained.

Man, doesn't that sound like so many churches today? They want the award-winning bands, celebrity preachers, feel-good messages, and flashy Jesus. How many churches would empty if what Jesus fully preached was *actually* taught and not cherry-picked?

If we follow Jesus, we're told, "If anyone would come after Me, he must deny himself and take up his cross and follow Me" (Matthew 16:24). When you become a "Christian" and nothing in your life has changed—if you're still drinking, drugging, sexing, and the rest, are you truly following Jesus and His teachings? Have you taken up your cross?

Christianity comes with a cost. When I say "yes" to Jesus, I say "no" to abortion, I say "no" to supporting gay marriage, I say "no" to non-Biblical divorce, and more.

All of that being said, yes, Jesus is just as controversial today as He was 2,000 years ago.

So look deep in your heart: are you carrying your cross each and every day and following the teachings of Biblical Jesus, or have you set it down and accepted the Jesus of this "New Christianity," because only one of them can be the real Jesus. Can the real Jesus please stand up?

But maybe you don't fully understand it, yet, and that's okay. You might be thinking, "Tim, why? Why would I give up everything I enjoy to follow *this* Jesus? What can He do for me? What has He done for you?"

Well, let me tell you about my best friend Jesus . . .

I've been a "Christian" since I was six-years-old; I put "Christian" in quotes here because although I would say I was a Christian, went to church regularly, and prayed, I don't think I really learned what it meant to be a Christian until just a couple years ago.

Like I stated earlier, I grew up in a dysfunctional house around generational alcoholism and codependency; by stating that, a lot of you know exactly where I'm coming from—tremendous amounts of pain, confusion, anxiety, and hurt.

Growing up in that environment, I would always say, "I'm not going to let alcoholism affect me." I was going to live a life in spite of it; no matter what, family alcoholism wasn't going to hold me back.

Little did I know it was already affecting me: it affected how I related to others, myself, and God.

I learned to internalize everything. Instead of naturally displaying emotions and finding release, I buried everything. At a young age, I learned "don't talk, think, or feel." Everything stayed inside and festered, like bubbling acid in my stomach. In my house, I never learned how to deal with life in a healthy way.

To some degree, up until a couple years ago, I dealt with anxiety unhealthily my entire life. I remember extreme nervousness before soccer practices, school days, and sometimes even just going out to see friends. My anxiety was mixed with perfectionism, which I learned from my childhood as well—act perfect, be perfect, and no one will know what goes on behind closed doors.

Fast forward to when I'm twenty-seven; I had just graduated grad school, was on the job hunt, and it didn't take long for me to figure out life wasn't going how I thought it would. I had a plan for my life; it was all *perfectly* planned out: I was going to get my thesis published, get a job teaching college students, do some book readings across the U.S., and it was all going to be great.

But none of that happened. The life I had envisioned and planned for was impossible—and completely void of God.

My life stopped, and that's not a metaphor. For all of you reading this dealing with mental illness (anxiety, depression, and the like), you know what I'm talking about. You want to do things, but you can't; you want to get a job, a house, get married, but your body and mind scream at you, "No!" You feel like a prisoner to yourself, shackled and tossed overboard.

JESUS

It was honestly Hell on earth for me. I couldn't see an hour—let alone a day—ahead. My mind was trapped in the moment: "I have anxiety. I feel panic. When will this go away?" Over and over on a loop, day in and day out. I dreaded going to sleep, because when I'd wake up, I'd wake up trembling and so full of fear. I couldn't eat; I literally had zero appetite. I lost twenty pounds in a matter of weeks. I drank protein shakes to try and get calories in my body. I was there—present in my body—but everything happening around me was out of control.

And that's when I hit rock-bottom. I didn't believe I could ever be healed. What I was going through was just going to be my new life, and that was what it was going to be forever. My mind was completely against me. I was terribly sad and lost. Deep in my mind, I heard, "You can end this. Get in your car, get on the highway, and jump into traffic."

It's so hard to describe why your own mind would tell you that. Darkness had a grip on me and was squeezing tight. I had no answers and no hope.

Through the grace of God, and by reaching out to family, friends, and professionals, I survived.

Then I contacted a Christian counselor and started doing the work.

Friends, if you're reading this, you've survived your hardest days and hardest moments. Never forget that. Through God, you're stronger than you know, and no weapon formed against you will prosper (Isaiah 54:17).

Early on in counseling, I had a legitimate life-changing moment when my counselor (Matt) and I went over the story of Cain and Abel in Genesis chapter 4. Matt described how Cain and Abel each brought God an offering; one of their offerings was acceptable and the other's wasn't. Matt then asked what I was offering God.

That question changed my life: "What are you offering God?"

What was I giving God? Up until that point, my life had been about me and what I wanted. I wanted a published book, a tenure contract, recognition, and praise. But what was I giving? Where did God fit in?

My life had been a throne to myself. I was always after that next award or accomplishment, and I always wanted more. That's where my worth came from; I didn't allow my worth to come from God. I had gotten everything so backward.

I was constantly striving for that next thing, but I never stopped to let Jesus' love for me be enough. I didn't realize I was created with worth. I kept seeking worth from others and what they thought, but I had completely missed how much worth I already had; Jesus had said, "You are worth this much" when He spread His arms out on the cross.

God doesn't need my book, my money, or my status—He doesn't need any of that. What He desires, though, is *me* . . . and you. He wants my heart to be for Him and to serve Him and to give Him all the praise in every victory. Nothing I do should be about me; it should all point to Him.

I needed to surrender what my idea of success was and accept God's plan for me, a plan of hope and a future through Him. Because no matter what I did or what I would do or accomplish, it was never going to be enough for me. Instead, Jesus said, "You're already enough, just the way you are—*because of Me.*"

Brother and sister, you're enough. You don't need to get that promotion, get sober, or reconcile with family. You don't need to attend church every week, donate a paycheck, or put out that cigarette. Should you do all of those things, if the Bible says "yes," then yes, but you don't need to accomplish anything more to receive Jesus' love. He loves you right where you're at.

He loved me at my lowest, when I had nothing and could give Him nothing. He loves you right where you're at, too.

Knowing all the sins I would make in this world, all the screw ups and failures, Jesus died for me anyway, and because of that love—that miraculous, bursting, unthinkable love—that's why I know I can release full control of my life to Him. I can release control and follow His plan for me, because He already showed me how much He loved me on the cross, and He continues to show how much He loves me each and every day.

JESUS

I fully rededicated my life to Christ May 7, 2016. I got on my knees before God and made a decision: no matter what, because I trusted Him, I was going to release control. I was going to let go of control over my career, anxiety, family, and relationships. I was going to trust Him, because He loved me first (1 John 4:19).

For me, that moment of surrender was about as sweet as life can get.

My grandpa once told a story of how he almost drowned when he was a boy. He was walking across a frozen lake when the ice broke and he fell through. That frigid lake tried to take him, but his dad was there to save him from a watery grave.

In my own life, I was drowning. I was being overtaken. I couldn't keep my head above water any longer. I cried out and said, "Jesus, I need You to save me." And did He save me? He sure did.

That's the Jesus I know and want to share with you. Because of His love for me, I'm willing to follow Him and His teachings. He loves me, passionately pursues me, and will never abandon me, even in my darkest moments. And what's more, He's restored me; He's given me back the years the locusts have eaten (Joel 2:25).

Now, I try to chase after Him in all things—I continually put myself on the altar and ask where He would have me go and what He would have me do, I lead my family out of His guidance and not my suggestions, and I deliberately follow Him through the rest. He is firmly the King of my life, and because He is, I have no fear. He's got this.

I'm a child of His and I am unashamed; He saved me from myself.

He's ready for you to surrender all at His feet, too—each day, moment, and struggle. Let Him be Lord over your life. You'll *never* regret it. You'll know a love and wholeness this world *cannot* offer.

His love and way of life is offensive to our sinful selves, but let Him overtake you and show you something new.

> Then one of the elders said to me, "Do not weep! See, the Lion of the tribe of Judah, the Root of David, has triumphed." (Revelation 5:5a)

The Most Offensive Book Ever Written

Jesus has triumphed. Amen.

In Closing

When Jesus arrived in Jerusalem, a week before His death, He was greeted with palm branches and shouts of "Hosanna," a word which can be translated as a term of adoration, respect, and praise. The complete story can be found in Matthew 21.

As Jesus entered Jerusalem, Matthew tells us "a very large crowd spread their cloaks on the road, while others cut branches from the trees and spread them on the road" (Matthew 21:8). However, this joyful story takes a somber turn with what Luke adds in his gospel: Luke says, "As He [Jesus] approached Jerusalem and saw the city, He wept over it" (Luke 19:41). Studying the verse and context a bit more, I wonder if why Jesus wept was this: these "believers" in Jerusalem who gathered and shouted "Hosanna" and put their cloaks on the road, would be the same people within a week who would be shouting, "Crucify Him! Crucify Him!" (Luke 23:21).

For Jesus, knowing what was coming, how crushing. When He was on trial, before His crucifixion, I wonder if He looked out at the crowd and recognized some of the same people who had laid their cloaks down.

Early believers were expecting the Messiah to come to Jerusalem and rescue the city with sword and shield. Jesus came to rescue the city, but instead of war, He brought eternal peace and salvation. The people didn't want that; they wanted more. Jesus—their Messiah—didn't reach their expectations, so they had Him killed.

The Most Offensive Book Ever Written

If Jesus was alive today and preaching the *same* words He did during His earthly ministry (words on Hell, divorce, murder, and everything else we covered in this book), how many "Christians" would turn their backs on Him and want Him canceled, embarrassed, and forgotten?

Some estimate there are a billion "Christians" in the world. But how many of these so-called Christians are actually Bible-based, God fearing, commandment following Christians—Christians that actually live differently than the rest of the world? I fear when I predict that number might be close to one in ten.

In writing this book, was my goal to judge, be called a "bigot," be canceled, and revel in insulting others? No. In getting this book published, I don't know what the cost will be, but I know there will be a cost on some level: I may lose friends, get horrible hate mail, one star reviews, and name-called. Knowing all of that going in, why did I write this book?

I wrote it for us—Christians. As much as there is an emotional cost to me in getting this book published, it's time we all understand there is a cost to being a Christian. Romans 6:1 and 2 says, "What shall we say then? Shall we go on sinning so that grace may increase? By no means! We died to sin; how can we live in it any longer?"

True, Bible-based Christians: we are not of this world, so we need to start acting like it! It's time we start living differently.

"I love Jesus, but I still don't see what's wrong with homosexuality, gay marriage, abortion, other religions, and the rest." Then do you really love Jesus and what He stood for and spoke on, or do you love this soft, make-believe Jesus that "New Christianity" is pushing. If God didn't care one way or the other, He would have said that. He wouldn't have spent 66 books showing us how to live and *why*.

I hope you heard the "why" in each section. It's not only the Bible saying "Homosexuality = Bad" or "Abortion = Bad." No. God's "why" is what makes all the difference. He wants what is best for you and your family and your children, and He wants to nourish your faith and bless your future generations. God's laws were

In Closing

given not to punish, but to bless. Let me repeat that in case you in the back were checking your phone and missed it: God's laws were given not to punish, but to bless. His Word comes from a place of love, not hate.

It's easy to say, "Well, Christians hate gays, adulterers, and addicts," but that is a clumsy argument and a sweepingly ignorant absolute. True Christians hate the sin, but have strong compassion for the sinner, because each one of us is the sinner. We each nailed Jesus to the tree, but even on the cross, He found love and mercy for those crucifying Him (Luke 23:34).

As our time together comes to a close, I want to leave you all with two challenges:

My first challenge is for the leaders of churches, groups, and ministries out there: Leaders, teach it—teach the Bible *in its entirety*. Milky, wishy-washy, liberal Christianity doesn't transform lives; God's Word—Biblical truth through Jesus Christ—changes lives.

"But our congregants won't like it." In the previous section, we went over how truckloads of disciples left Jesus. He didn't care about numbers. Christianity isn't about making people feel good; Christianity is about radical transformation and unbelievable redemption, and that's the bottom line.

I would rather have a church with fifty people that come every week because they want to be challenged, hear the truth, and live the way they're called to, than a church with 25,000 people who come to get a pat on the back and then return to their regular lives, absent of God, for the next six days.

I attended a Christmas service a couple years ago, and I honestly don't remember much of the service, but I remember the pastor's prayer. While praying, Pastor Dan said, "Help us go into this New Year and live boldly." I don't know why that stuck out to me at the time, but so many times since I've remembered that: live boldly.

Leaders, live boldly, bravely, and Biblically. Draw the line in the sand. Examine what you're teaching, and just as importantly, examine *why* you're teaching it. Are you teaching what you're teaching because it'll keep people coming back, it won't ruffle any feathers, it's a good lesson that's adequate enough, or are you teaching what you're teaching because it's fiercely true, challenging to societal norms, and exactly what Jesus would teach if He was on that stage?

Do you think Jesus would hold back? Do you think He'd care how much money got put in the basket each week? Do you think He'd care about how full the parking lot was? Do you think He'd teach fluff to make the masses feel good? Having read through the gospels, my answer would be "no" to every single one of those questions.

Leaders, somewhere along the lines, it became more about numbers than it did about the Message.

Fix it.

My second challenge encompasses all of us: Christians, let's live it.

"But I only agree with some of that. I don't agree with everything in this book." Then, by Biblical definition, you are not a true Christ follower. I have to be blunt here, because it's that important: If you choose to agree with the "drinking" and "abortion" stance, but not the "gay marriage" and "other religions" stance, then by definition you are not a Christ follower from a strictly Biblical perspective.

As far as Biblical truth goes—absolute Truth—there is no in-between. You're either a Christ follower or you're not; you either believe what the Bible says or you don't. There is a line and you have to pick a side. In Revelation 3:16, it says, "So, because you are lukewarm—neither hot nor cold—I am about to spit you out of my mouth." It's time to take a hard look at scripture and these topics and see if your beliefs are actually what is spoken and preached in the Bible.

And let me say this one last time: I get it; some of these can be hard to agree with and we want to show love and support to everyone no matter what they do or how they live their lives, but that is simply not what the Bible teaches.

At the end of the day, whatever Jesus taught is good enough for me, and that's why I believe it. He wants what is best for me, He has plans for me, and He loves me. Period.

In Closing

"But—" But nothing. We don't get to change what God wrote. He said it and that's it. Knowing that, I also know God's character—a character of love, grace, and peace. Because I know God, I will believe His words until the end of time, and nothing can make me change them.

It's time we live His Word and, friends, the time to live it is now. In the U.S., less people are going to church and reading their Bibles than ever before. Now, more than ever, it's important to know what the Bible says and why you believe what you believe.

Tony Evans, a fantastic preacher out of Dallas, has been talking on this topic, and he recently called Christians "the away team." That's where we are in Western society. Government is caring less and less about us, schools are pushing their own agendas, free speech is going out the window, and bringing it all back to the thesis of this book: the Bible is becoming more and more offensive each and every day.

And rightfully so. The Bible *is* offensive: it's an inclusive Book (for everybody) with an exclusive outlook (to those who actually live its words and take them to heart). The Bible says what is right and what is wrong. It gives laws on how to live. It says "no" and throws down restrictions. But it does all of these things out of love. No other book can say that.

Because so many find the Bible offensive to their lifestyle, it's on a list to be canceled, that I can guarantee. The war on Christianity is being ramped up year after year; just look at what is being talked about in society now compared to ten years ago, and it won't end in my lifetime. I believe it will only get worse until the final days.

Listen to what Jesus says in Matthew 24, speaking on the end times:

> You will hear of wars and rumors of wars, but see to it that you are not alarmed. Such things must happen, but the end is still to come. Nation will rise against nation, and kingdom against kingdom. There will be famines and earthquakes in various places. All these are the beginning of birth pains. Then you will be handed over to

be persecuted and put to death, and you will be hated by all nations because of Me. At that time many will turn away from the faith and will betray and hate each other, and many false prophets will appear and deceive many people. Because of the increase in wickedness, the love of most will grow cold, but he who stands firm to the end will be saved (verses 6–13).

The time is coming when all Christians will have to pick a side: which team are you on? Will you turn away from your faith and abandon Christianity for some more culturally acceptable "iety" or "ology," or will you stand firm and be persecuted for your belief and faith in the one true God, even if it means unto death?

Whether you realize it or not, the persecution of Christians is nothing new. Organizations I'm proud to support, The Voice of the Martyrs and Open Doors, tell the stories of persecuted Christians in countries all over the world. Afghanistan, China, Nigeria, and North Korea are just a couple countries where extreme persecution takes place on a daily basis. Christians are being imprisoned, tortured, enslaved, and even killed because of their faith in Jesus. Those believers are not believing in some watered-down version of Christianity, this "New Christianity," but in true Christianity that is offensive, brutally honest, and life-changing.

Pray for our persecuted brothers and sisters as if you were with them (Hebrews 13:3), because when our time comes, we'll want their prayers, too.

The Bible is holy and so are its truths. It can stand on its own against societal correctness; God doesn't need us to make the Bible more attractive by tainting it with our worldview (Matthew 24:35). Jesus is what is attractive; not our PC BS. Who are we to think God needs us to change His Word to make it more acceptable and palatable? You know what God really needs? For us to get out of His way.

There's an old hymn called "I Have Decided to Follow Jesus." It's about a believer's faith walk in constant pursuit of Christ, no matter what. The second verse of the song has these words, a challenge for us today: "Though none go with me, still I will follow."

In Closing

Being a Biblical Christian isn't popular by societal standards. It won't get you a big promotion, an invite to an exclusive party, or even a pat on the back. In fact, to much of society, Biblical Christianity will give you the exact opposite: it'll get you snubbed, ignored, name-called, and maybe even worst of all (by their standards)—canceled.

No matter what, though, friends, continue to follow and pursue Him. If none follow, if none encourage, if none lift you up in prayer, press on for Him. Run the race for Him (2 Timothy 4:7). It will all be worth it—a million times over. Of this I'm sure.

Society can cancel you, but Jesus will never be stopped, and our Spirit will never be silenced.

Let this be our battle cry, brothers and sisters: *Though none go with me, still I will follow.*

Praying for you all, always.

> Let us not become weary in doing good, for at the proper time we will reap a harvest if we do not give up. (Galatians 6:9)

Acknowledgements

I'm grateful to my Lord and Savior, Jesus Christ. You have blessed me with gifts and talents beyond measure, and I so enjoy using them to glorify You; I hope they bring You pleasure and praise each and every day. Let me continue to fight daily to keep myself on the altar and not back down.

I'm thankful to my wife. Natalie, thank you for your creativity, investment, and desire to pursue God *together*, as a unified front. The best is yet to come, in this life and the next.

I'm thankful to my daughter. You're not even born yet, but you're already pushing me to be a man you'd be proud of. May I always work at being the best dad for you.

I'm thankful to my counselor, Matt. Thank you for your wisdom and guidance in helping me get to a place of sanity. I don't know where I would be without you.

I'm thankful to my mom, dad, brother, and sister. I'm grateful for all of your continued support and encouragement. I've learned so much being raised in this family and I wouldn't change it for anything.

I'm thankful to my extended family, as well. Thank you all for your joy, laughter, and love.

I want to call out my Grandpa McIlveen. Gramps, because you found God, I found God. You were a blessing to your children, their children, and now their children's children. We all know better, and may all the men in the family strive to be half the man, father, husband, and Christian you were. We miss you so much.

For my persecuted brothers and sisters around the world: Your belief in the face of extreme adversity is not only courageous, but deeply inspiring. May you all be blessed abundantly, and may I somehow manage to grasp a fraction of your zealous faith. "I will live for Christ or I will die for Christ, but I will never turn back."

I'm grateful to my English and writing teachers throughout my educational career, including Mort Castle, Christian TeBordo, Kyle Beachy, Gary Johnson, and others. Because of your investment in me, I can invest in others. Thank you.

There are so many great speakers and writers I need to thank for their inspiration on this project: Tony Evans, Lee Strobel, Gary Thomas, Patrick Henry Reardon, John Piper, Ron Phillips, Colin S. Smith, Bill Wiese, A.W. Tozer, and C.S. Lewis. You are all giants and I'm only standing on your shoulders.

Lastly, but not least, I want to thank *you*—the reader. Thank you for your time in reading this work of mine. We went over some really hard topics, but I'm grateful to have been able to share with you. As always, you can reach out to me directly at timdustinwrites@gmail.com and keep up to date with all my writing/speaking/miscellaneous news at TimDustinWrites.com

Praying for you all on your faith journey, for your family, and for your children's children. May God reveal His blessings to you as you stand and live out your Biblical Christianity.

Live boldly, act bravely, and pray deeply. No matter the cost.

> The Lord bless you and keep you; the Lord make His face shine upon you and be gracious to you; the Lord turn His face toward you and give you peace. (Numbers 6:24–26)

www.ingramcontent.com/pod-product-compliance
Lightning Source LLC
Chambersburg PA
CBHW070521100426
42743CB00010B/1895